Bioethics and the Character of Human Life

Bioethics and the Character of Human Life

Essays and Reflections

GILBERT MEILAENDER

CASCADE *Books* · Eugene, Oregon

BIOETHICS AND THE CHARACTER OF HUMAN LIFE
Essays and Reflections

Cascade Books
An Imprint of Wipf and Stock Publishers
199 W. 8th Ave., Suite 3
Eugene, OR 97401

www.wipfandstock.com

PAPERBACK ISBN: 978-1-7252-5128-1
HARDCOVER ISBN: 978-1-7252-5129-8
EBOOK ISBN: 978-1-7252-5130-4

Cataloguing-in-Publication data:

Names: Meilaender, Gilbert, 1946–, author.

Title: Bioethics and the character of human life : essays and reflections / Gilbert Meilaender.

Description: Eugene, OR : Cascade Books, 2020 | Includes bibliographical references and index.

Identifiers: ISBN 978-1-7252-5128-1 (paperback) | ISBN 978-1-7252-5129-8 (hardcover) | ISBN 978-1-7252-5130-4 (ebook)

Subjects: LCSH: Medical ethics—Religious aspects—Christianity. | Christian ethics.| Bioethics. | Bioethics—Religious aspects—Christianity.

Classification: R725.56 .M46 2020 (paperback) | R725.56 .M46 (ebook)

Manufactured in the U.S.A.   05/14/20

TO
LEON R. KASS
and
DAVID H. SMITH
My Unofficial Teachers

Contents

IV
Thinking Theologically:
To Be a Person

Preface

For roughly forty years I taught ethics (and bioethics) in the religion departments of several very different colleges and universities, but there were moments when I wished I had instead specialized in something very different—perhaps, say, texts and artifacts from the world of the ancient Near East. Had I done that, when I walked into the classroom day after day the students would have known that I was the expert and they were not. They would almost surely have lacked the skills that would have entitled them to an opinion about how an ancient Akkadian text ought to be translated. They would have been unable to identify ancient archaeological artifacts or say much about the kind of civilization in which such artifacts would have been found.

But decades ago the die was cast, and ethics it has been. To be sure, in certain ways I have some expertise that students recognize. But that expertise does little more than help all of us get clear on what we're thinking about. When we take the next step and ask "what we ought to think about what we're thinking about," students do not recognize me as an expert. Nor should they. We are all just human beings, doing our best to think about what being human means and what it requires of us.

This is surely true when we think about the kinds of issues taken up in the essays gathered together in this book. Although, as I will note below, the essays range widely and are of different sorts, in their own way they all take up issues in bioethics. And while it is true that bioethics has gradually become something resembling an academic discipline, and while it is true that some people are experts in the literature of that would-be discipline, the problems of bioethics are fundamentally human problems. That, in fact, is why they are so engaging to so many people. And when we try to decide what we ought to think about them, there are, in the end, no experts—just human beings wrestling with what it means to be human and what our humanity requires of us. Why this should be the case we can see from three related but slightly different angles.

First, many of the most significant issues in bioethics clearly invite us to think about our place in the universe, about the meaning of suffering, about the relation between our freedom and the natural and historical constraints that limit us, about the degree of altruism we can or should expect from others, about the meaning of human dignity, about the sense in which death is or is not an evil. These are not, finally, technical questions on which only experts may comment. They are questions about who we are, where we are going, and what sort of people we want to be. And because they concern the meaning of a genuinely human life, they are topics about which there will always be more than one view. They are the very stuff of democratic, social discourse. We should not want it any other way.

Second, to press the point a bit further, some of the most disputed issues in bioethics engage—sooner or later—what is perhaps the most fundamental question any society can face: Whose good counts in the common good? So, for example, our centuries-long attempt to recognize and honor human equality has been at the heart of arguments about an issue that has generated much public debate in recent years—namely, how we should regard and treat human embryos. Bioethics is caught within the tension between our eagerness to take advantage of the usefulness of embryos (both for research and for reproductive technologies) and our commitment to recognize and protect the weakest and most vulnerable of human lives. This can hardly be a matter for bioethicists alone to decide.

And third, if the first two points are valid, then we should not be eager to narrow our public discussion and reflection so much that it excludes ideas—even and especially religious ones—that do not command general agreement. There is a certain anxiety displayed in claims that public discussion about bioethical questions must not draw on beliefs that are part of larger religious or metaphysical comprehensive visions. Such claims manifest a nervousness that tries to fix in advance acceptable modes of argument, and they seem to suggest a quasi-religious hope for a politics from which conflict has been eliminated. But there will always be conflict about what is good for human beings, and there will always be more than one way to think about such matters. Moreover, it is not bad for us to learn that the world is sometimes contrary to what we will and desire. Bioethics will be most useful when, rather than picturing itself as the province of experts alone, it invites all of us to reflect on matters central to human life.

The essays collected here, though very different in many ways, seek to think about bioethics from that perspective. Many of them began as lectures or talks, morphed into journal or magazine articles, and now are drawn together here. Because of their different origins the essays took rather different forms, some with and others entirely without footnotes. Rather than trying to recapture and footnote every specific citation, and in the interest of having the essays take similar form here, I have split the difference by providing, at the end of each chapter, bibliographic references to the most important sources used in that chapter.

Inevitably, there is also some repetition here and there in the essays. One can find only so many ways to make a point, and sometimes a particular quotation may be too good to use only once. Thus, for example, anyone who reads these essays from start to finish will become acquainted with a passage from Ralph McInerny that I especially like, and will see the importance to me of an essay by Hans Jonas, and will observe the influence of Paul Ramsey and Oliver O'Donovan on my thinking. Readers will see certain emphases recurring along the way—the distinction between making and doing or between doing and accomplishing; the difference between what we intend to do and the foreseen but unintended results of our action; the significance of the body as the place of personal presence; the way in which religious beliefs quite rightly shape our thinking about fundamental moral questions and lie at the root of what it means to be a person. But, of course, many may not read from start to finish, nor is it necessary to do so. The essays can be taken up in almost any order.

The four essays in the first section ("Bioethics and Public Life"), although quite varied, all grow out of my experience as a member (from 2002 to 2009) of the President's Council on Bioethics. Indeed, it is unlikely any of them would have been written were it not for that experience. One of the essays reflects very directly on the experience and considers how a public bioethics commission might best be structured and what we should hope for from it. Another attempts to use some of the fruits of the Council's work to think in very specific theological terms about the morality of enhancing human traits and capacities.

The essays of the next two sections turn more directly to exploration of some bioethical problems that arise at the beginning and the end of life. However wide the range of bioethics has by now become, however wide its scope may become, it is surely true that the human significance of birth, death, marriage, and parenthood accounts in large part for the attention many people pay to bioethics.

The essays of the second section focus especially on the relation between the generations. There are certainly other important questions that arise at the beginning of life (most obviously, abortion). But these essays attend primarily to our desire to have children—and often to have children of a certain sort. As medicine's capacity to satisfy those desires increases, so do the moral quandaries that require our attention and reflection.

When we give birth to the next generation, we give birth to those who will succeed us. Life's beginning and life's ending are, therefore, closely related. The essays of the third section turn to questions about how we ought to live toward our dying, how much we should be willing to do to fend off that dying, how much control we ought to exercise over the moment of our death, and how medicine can best serve us at the end of life—questions none of us can entirely avoid.

The two essays in the fourth and last section approach bioethics much less directly. Each of them concerns itself with what it means to speak of someone as a "person." This is a question that has been of incalculable importance in bioethical issues at both the beginning and the end of life. The two essays eventually make similar forays into Christian teaching about the triune being of God; for, as it happens, that teaching has bequeathed to us an important understanding of what it means to be a person—an understanding very different from the concept of "personhood" that has played a major role in bioethics for the last half century.

In none of these essays do I imagine that I can or do offer the last word to be said on the issues discussed. But in all of them I do seek, as best I can, to offer reflection about bioethics that is distinctive in certain ways—not least in that I try to think within a thick and developed tradition of thought that is willing (even eager) to let our reflection be shaped by theological perspectives. Those who share such a perspective may, I hope, be helped to think further about its implications for bioethics. And those who do not may, I hope, at least gain a little more insight into a different way of thinking about issues that concern us all.

I

Bioethics and Public Life

1

Bioethics and the Character
of Human Life[1]

When the Hastings Center was founded in 1969 as the first bioethics "think tank" in the United States, it planned research in four areas of concern: death and dying (and efforts to overcome the limits of our finitude); behavior control (and the relation between human activities and the happiness attendant upon them); genetic screening, counseling, and engineering (including questions of kinship, procreation, and attitudes toward future generations); and population policy and family planning (which, at least implicitly, asked about the relation of our own time to future generations). If we add explicit attention to moral problems raised by human experimentation, the list could still today serve well as a brief itemization of the central concerns of bioethics. The reason these issues have been and continue to be central, and no doubt the reason bioethics has been an object of such lively public interest and concern, is obvious: These topics are not driven simply by concern for public policy regulations; rather, they involve some of the most important aspects of our humanity and raise some of the deepest questions about what it means to be human.

There is no neutral ground from which to discuss such questions. They are inevitably normative, value-laden, and metaphysical in character.

---

1. An earlier version of this essay appeared in *The New Atlantis* 1 (Spring 2003).

3

Our starting point, therefore, should not deny this. Our approach should not be that taken by the Human Embryo Research Panel (established by NIH in the mid-1990s), which characterized its stance as follows:

> Throughout its deliberations, the Panel considered the wide range of views held by American citizens on the moral status of preimplantation embryos. In recommending public policy, the Panel was not called upon to decide which of these views is correct. Rather, its task was to propose guidelines for preimplantation human embryo research that would be acceptable public policy based on reasoning that takes account of generally held public views regarding the beginning and development of human life. The Panel weighed arguments for and against Federal funding of this research in light of the best available information and scientific knowledge and conducted its deliberations in terms that were independent of a particular religious or philosophical perspective.

But, there are no such terms, and the public is not likely to believe such protestations of neutrality. We are not philosopher-kings who can adjudicate disputes between conflicting views without ourselves being parties to the argument. We are human beings, invited to reflect upon what that humanity means and requires in the field of bioethics.

In this essay I hope to invite such reflection and conversation. The essay explores, without attempting to resolve, some of the background issues that inevitably shape thought in bioethics. Acknowledging from the outset that much more might be said about any of them, I will unpack briefly four aspects of a truly human bioethics.

THE UNITY AND INTEGRITY OF THE HUMAN BEING

The beginning of wisdom in bioethics may lie in the effort to think about what human beings are and why it matters morally. From several different angles, medical advance has tempted us to lose sight of any sense in which the embodied human being is an integral, organic whole. We can illustrate this first by noting how advancing genetic knowledge encourages us to think of human beings as no more than collections of parts.

Consider the following sentences from Ernest Hemingway's *Old Man and the Sea*:

> He looked down into the water and watched the lines that went straight down into the dark of the water. He kept them straighter

4

than anyone did, so that at each level in the darkness of the stream there would be a bait waiting exactly where he wished it to be for any fish that swam there. . . . I have no understanding of it and I am not sure that I believe in it. Perhaps it was a sin to kill the fish. . . . He urinated outside the shack and then went up the road to wake the boy. He was shivering with the morning cold. . . . Then he was sorry for the great fish that had nothing to eat and his determination to kill him never relaxed in his sorrow for him. How many people will he feed, he thought. But are they worthy to eat him? . . . That was the saddest thing I ever saw with them, the old man thought. The boy was sad too and we begged her pardon and butchered her promptly. . . . The boy did not go down. He had been there before and one of the fishermen was looking after the skiff for him.

To read this passage as I have printed it here makes almost no sense; yet, each individual sentence is clear and is not hard to understand. The reason is a simple one. The sentences, though all from the same book, are drawn at random from pages 29, 104–5, 22, 74, 48, and 123—in that order.

This is not unlike the way we sometimes characterize our humanity in an age of rapid advances in genetic knowledge. Consider, for example, the following passage from biologist Thomas Eisner, cited by Mary Midgley:

> As a consequence of recent advances in genetic engineering, [a biological species] must be viewed as . . . a depository of genes that are potentially transferable. A species is not merely a hard-bound volume of the library of nature. It is also a loose-leaf book, whose individual pages, the genes, might be available for selective transfer and modification of other species.

I have used *The Old Man and the Sea* to illustrate this, splicing together sentences from different parts of the book—and the result is something almost entirely unintelligible. And suppose I were also to splice in sentences from *Pride and Prejudice* and *The Kid from Tompkinsville*. We would then have an artifact we could not even name. As a book is not an artifact whose pages can simply be moved around willy-nilly, so also a human being is not what Eisner called "a depository of genes that are potentially transferable." We might try to think of human beings (or the other animals) in that way, and, indeed, we are often invited to think of them as collections of genes (or as collections of organs possibly available for transplant), but we might also wonder whether in doing so we lose a sense of ourselves as integrated, organic wholes.

Integrality of persons

5

Even if we think of the human being as an integrated organism, the nature of its unity remains puzzling in a second way. The seeming duality of person and body has played a significant role in bioethics. As the language of "personhood" gradually came to prominence in bioethical reflection, attention has often been directed to circumstances in which the duality of body and person seems pronounced. Suppose a child is born who, throughout his life, will be profoundly retarded. Or suppose an elderly woman has now become severely demented. Suppose because of trauma a person lapses into a permanent vegetative state. How shall we describe such human beings? Is it best to say that they are no longer persons? Or is it more revealing to describe them as severely disabled persons? Similar questions arise with embryos and fetuses. Are they human organisms that have not yet attained personhood? Or are they the weakest and most vulnerable of human persons?

Related questions arise when we think of conditions often, but controversially, regarded as disabilities. Those who are deaf and have learned to sign perhaps create and constitute a culture of their own, a manualist as opposed to an oralist culture. If so, one might argue that they are disabled only in an oralist culture, even as those who hear but do not sign would be disabled if placed in the midst of a manualist culture. So long as the deaf are able to function at a high level within that manualist culture, does it matter in what way they function? Notice that the harder we press such views the less significant becomes any normative human form. A head, or a brain, might be sufficient, if it could find ways to carry out at a high level the functions important to our life.

Such puzzles are inherent in the human condition, and they are sufficiently puzzling that we may struggle to find the right language in which to discuss that aspect of the human being which cannot be reduced to body. Within the unity of the human being a duality remains, and I will here use the language of "spirit" to gesture toward it. As embodied spirits (or inspirited bodies) we stand at the juncture of nature and spirit, tempted by reductionisms of various sorts. We have no access to the spirit—the person—apart from the body, which is the place of personal presence; yet, we are deeply ill at ease in the presence of a living human body from which all that is personal seems absent. It is fair to say, I think, that, in reflecting upon the duality of our nature, we have traditionally given a kind of primacy to the living human body. Thus, uneasy as we might be with the living body from which the person seems absent, we would be very reluctant indeed to bury that body while its heart still beats.

In any case, the problems of bioethics force us to ask what a human being really is and, in doing so, to reflect upon the unity and integrity of the human person. We must think about the moral meaning of the living human body—whether it exists simply as an interchangeable collection of parts, whether it exists merely as a carrier for what really counts (the personal realm of mind or spirit), whether a living human being who lacks cognitive, personal qualities is no longer one of us or is simply the weakest and most needy one of us.

FINITUDE AND FREEDOM

In one of his delightful essays, collected in *The Medusa and the Snail*, the late Lewis Thomas explores the deeply buried origins of our word *hybrid*. It comes from the Latin *hybrida*, the name for the offspring of a wild boar and a domestic sow. But in its more distant origins the word, as Thomas puts it, "carries its own disapproval inside." Its more distant etymological ancestor is the Greek *hubris*, insolence against the gods. That is, buried somewhere in the development of our language is a connection between two beings unnaturally joined together and human usurping of the prerogatives of the gods. Thomas summarizes his excursion into etymology as follows: "This is what the word has grown into, a warning, a code word, a shorthand signal from the language itself: if man starts doing things reserved for the gods, deifying himself, the outcome will be something worse for him, symbolically, than the litters of wild boars and domestic sows were for the Romans."

That is only one side of the matter, however. For Thomas can also write in a provocative paragraph,

> Is there something fundamentally unnatural, or intrinsically wrong . . . in the ambition that drives us all to reach a comprehensive understanding of nature, including ourselves? I cannot believe it. It would seem to be a more unnatural thing . . . for us to come on the same scene endowed as we are with curiosity . . . and then for us to do nothing about it or, worse, to try to suppress the questions. This is the greater danger for our species, to try to pretend . . . that we do not need to satisfy our curiosity. . . .

Using some old religious language, we might say that Thomas sees how, given the duality of our nature, we may go wrong in either of two ways: pride or sloth. As prideful beings, we may strive to be all freedom—acknowledging no limits to our creativity, supposing that our wisdom is sufficient to master the world. As slothful beings, we may timidly fear freedom and ignore the lure of new possibilities. Either is a denial of something essential to being human, a reduction of the full meaning of our humanity. Clearly, Thomas is inclined to fear most the dangers of sloth, but that may be only the mark in him of a passing modernity.

In any case, the duality of body and person is clearly related to what we may call a duality of finitude and freedom. The human being is the place where freedom and finitude meet; hence, it will always contravene something significant in our humanity to act as if we were *really* only free personal spirit or only finite body. Yet, because of the two-sidedness of our nature, we can look at a human being from each of these angles.

Drop me from the top of a fifty-story building and the law of gravity takes over, just as it does if we drop a rock; for as finite beings, we are located in space and time and subject to the laws of nature. But to some degree we are also free—able to some extent to transcend the seeming limits of nature and history. Therefore, as I fall from that fifty-story building, there is more to be said about my experience than can be said in terms of laws that deal with mass and velocity. For *this* falling object, after all, is also a self-aware subject. That I can know myself as a falling object means that I can to some extent distance my*self* from that falling object and cannot simply be equated with it. I am that falling object, yet I am also free from it. The crucial question, of course, is whether there is any limit to such free self-transcendence—whether we are, in fact, wise enough and good enough to be free self-creators or whether we should acknowledge any destructive possibilities in a freedom that refuses any limit.

Understanding our nature in this way, we can appreciate how hard it may be to evaluate advances in medicine, claims about the importance (or even obligatory quality) of research, attempts to enhance our nature in various ways, or efforts to master death. If we simply oppose the forward thrust of scientific medicine, we fail to honor human freedom. The zealous desire to know, to probe the secrets of nature, to combat disease—all that is an expression of our freedom from the limits of the given. Yet, of course, if we never find reason to stop in this restless attempt at mastery, we may fail to honor the human—and limited—character of our wisdom and virtue.

8

There is probably no cookbook that gives the recipe for knowing how best to honor—simultaneously—both our freedom and our finitude. That there ought to be limits to our freedom does not mean that we can easily state them in advance. But a truly human bioethics will recognize not only the creative but also the destructive possibilities in the exercise of our freedom.

THE RELATION BETWEEN THE GENERATIONS

Because we are not only free but are also embodied spirits, the biological and genetic bonds that connect the generations have moral meaning for us. We occupy a fixed place in the generations of humankind. Both Jews and Christians inculcate a command that calls upon us to honor our father and mother. It is a puzzling duty: to show gratitude for a bond in which we find ourselves without ever having freely chosen it. Yet, of course, insofar as the child is a gift, we might say that father and mother have also not chosen this bond. They too simply find themselves in it. A truly limitless freedom to make and remake ourselves, to pursue our projects in the world, would divorce us from the lines of kinship and descent that locate and identify us. Would that be the fulfillment of our nature? Or alienation from it?

It is, I think, fair to say that several different aspects of medical advance—in reproductive technologies, in psychopharmacology, in genetic screening, and one day perhaps in techniques for genetic enhancement or cloning—have made it more difficult for both parents and children simply to honor and affirm the bond between the generations and accept as a gift the lines of kinship that locate and identify them.

In his poem "After Making Love We Hear Footsteps," Galway Kinnell gives us a captivating image of young Fergus plopping down into bed between his parents: a "blessing love gives again into our arms." That image—of the child as a blessing, a gift that is the fruition not of an act of rational will but an act of love—can be contrasted with an image of the child as the parents' project or product. For the latter way of thinking, having a child becomes a project we undertake to satisfy our purposes and make our life complete. And, of course, our desire may be not simply for a child but for a child of a certain sex, a child with certain characteristics or capacities. Human cloning, were it possible, would from one angle bring to completion this image of the next generation as a product of rational will, undertaken to fulfill our desires. From another angle, of course, cloning

Do children "fulfill parents' desires"?

9

might be thought to break entirely the bond between the generations, since in the instance of cloning we do not even know how to name the relation between progenitor and offspring.

Pondering how best to think about the relation between the generations, we are driven once again to questions about when we should use our freedom to seek mastery or control and when, by contrast, we should accept certain limits inherent in human bodily life. The twentieth century began with considerable confidence in the possibility for eugenic control of the relation between the generations. That confidence suffered eclipse in the face of revelations of Nazi eugenic experiments, but it has reemerged in quite different ways. Today, any state-sponsored eugenic ideology would surely face considerable opposition in our society, but there is far more support for those who (to use the barbarous locution now common) "privatize" eugenic decisions.

Here again, there is no simple recipe for making decisions. Parents must indeed exercise reason and will to shape their children's lives. They do not and should not simply accept as given whatever disabilities, sufferings, or (even just) disappointments come their children's way. Still, as every child realizes at some point, the conscientious parent's effort to nurture and enhance can be crushing. It can make it difficult to accept the child who has been given, impossible to say simply, "It's good that you exist."

The implications for the bond between the generations become still more far-reaching when we consider that research may make possible alteration of the human germline. More than seventy-five years ago, without any precise knowledge of such intervention, C. S. Lewis contemplated such eugenic efforts, and in *The Abolition of Man* he noted the salient point that relates to my theme here: "What we call Man's power over Nature turns out to be a power exercised by some men over other men with Nature as its instrument." Alterations in the human germline would be an awesome exercise of human freedom and, if used in the struggle against disease, might promise (over time) a cure not only for individual sufferers but also for the human species. Yet, of course, the exercise of freedom is also an exercise of power, and just as—synchronically—parents need to allow the mystery of humanity to unfold in the lives of their children, so also—diachronically—one generation needs to allow others their freedom. How we sort out these competing goods will reveal much about how we understand the character of human life.

SUFFERING AND VULNERABILITY

Part of the sadness of human life is that we sometimes cannot and other times ought not do for others what they fervently desire. With respect to the relief of suffering, the great quest of modern research medicine, this is also true. Some relief we simply are unable to provide, a fact that only gives greater impetus to our efforts to discover causes and cures. It is precisely the fact of our inability to help in the face of great suffering that fuels the research "imperative" of which we are all beneficiaries. Nevertheless, it is important to ask how overriding this imperative is—whether there are means to the possible relief of suffering that we ought not take up, and whether it would be good if we were not vulnerable to suffering.

So great is our modern concern to overcome suffering, we may almost forget that there are perspectives from which this goal is deliberately made secondary. For anyone drawn to Stoic philosophy, for example, bodily suffering could not finally be of great significance. It can harm us only if we are deceived into supposing that anything other than one's own inner self-mastery really counts. Thus, Seneca tells the story of Stilbo, whose country was captured, whose children and wife were lost, and who "as he emerged from the general desolation alone and yet happy, spoke as follows to Demetrius, called Sacker of Cities because of the destruction he brought upon them, in answer to the question whether he had lost anything: 'I have all my goods with me!'" And Seneca's comment demonstrates the power of Stoicism:

> There is a brave and stout-hearted man for you! The enemy con-
> quered, but Stilbo conquered his conqueror. "I have lost nothing!"
> Aye, he forced Demetrius to wonder whether he himself had con-
> quered after all. "My goods are all with me!" In other words, he
> deemed nothing that might be taken from him to be a good.

While it may be hard sometimes not to be repelled by the harshness of such Stoic vision, it is equally hard not to recognize the nobility of an outlook that makes how we live more important than how long. And if it seems to denigrate too much the goods of everyday life, we can detect a similar nobility in another ancient worldview that does not think these ordinary goods of no account.

During St. Augustine's life the cult of the martyrs continued to be of profound importance to average Christians, for persecution was still a recent memory. Augustine, therefore, was often required to preach at festivals of the martyrs. Commenting on some of these sermons of Augustine, first preached in the year 397 but newly discovered only in 1990, Peter Brown observed that the martyrs were the great heroes, the "muscular athletes" and "triumphant stars" of the faith. Nevertheless, Brown believed that in these sermons one can see Augustine quite deliberately making the feasts of the martyrs "less dramatic, so as to stress the daily drama of God's workings in the heart of the average Christian." Those average believers did not doubt that the grace of God had been spectacularly displayed in the courage of the martyrs. What they thought unlikely, however, was that such heroism could be displayed in their own less dramatic and more ordinary lives. So Augustine points "away from the current popular ideology of the triumph of the martyrs to the smaller pains and triumphs of daily life."

"God has many martyrs in secret," Augustine tells his hearers. "Some times you shiver with fever: you are fighting. You are in bed: it is you who are the athlete." Brown comments,

> Exquisite pain accompanied much late-Roman medical treatment. Furthermore, everyone, Augustine included, believed that amulets provided by skilled magicians . . . did indeed protect the sufferer— but at the cost of relying on supernatural powers other than Christ alone. They worked. To neglect them was like neglecting any other form of medicine. But the Christian must not use them. Thus, for Augustine to liken a Christian sickbed to a scene of martyrdom was not a strained comparison.

Here again—though in a way of life that will be, in some respects, quite different from Stoicism—one sees an outlook for which relief of suffering, however desired and desirable, is not the overriding imperative of life.

The Stoics remind us that an authentically human life may prize good-ness more than happiness and, indeed, that true virtue may be achieved precisely when we seem most vulnerable to suffering. The ancient Christians remind us that one might value competing goods (such as faithfulness to God) more highly than relief of suffering.

In the modern world we may admire such views, but we tend to keep our distance from them. The quest for health (or is it Health?), the attempt to master nature in service of human need and to refuse to accept the body's vulnerability to suffering, has characterized the modern age. If such a world offers less occasion for the display of nobility, it does not despise the sufferings of countless ordinary people—and that is no small gain. The research that makes such gains possible is greatly to be desired, but is it also imperative? Many questions of bioethics, especially of research, invite us to try to determine the difference between the desirable and the imperative.

One of the now classic essays in bioethics, first published in 1969, was Hans Jonas's "Philosophical Reflections on Experimenting with Human Subjects." It articulated at the very outset of the development of bioethics a difference between the desirable and the imperative. Jonas noted that sometimes it is imperative that a society avoid disaster; hence, we conscript soldiers to fight. The fact that we do not (ordinarily) conscript experimental subjects indicates that, however much we value the improvements to life made possible by medical research, we do not think of ourselves as having an obligation to make such improvements. Research brings betterment of our life; it does not save our society. It serves health—not Health.

Because this is true, we seek volunteers, not conscripts, in the cause of medical progress. And because this is true, far from using those who might be most readily available as handy research subjects, we should be most reluctant to use them. Indeed, Jonas defended "the inflexible principle that utter helplessness demands utter protection." That is, the vulnerability that ought to concern us most is not our own vulnerability to illness and suffering but, rather, the vulnerability of those whose very helplessness might make them seem all too readily available to us in our never-ending struggle to make progress. If "utter helplessness demands utter protection," we will have to ask ourselves whether it is right to build our medical progress upon the sacrificed lives of those—such as spare embryos—who seem expendable because doomed to die anyway.

Finally, we must also ask ourselves whether there might be research that is neither imperative nor desirable. If goodness is to be prized more than happiness, the endless quest to remake and enhance human life, to overcome vulnerability, may destroy other, equally important goods of an authentically human life. We recognize this truth, for example, in our role as parents. Conscientious parents want with all their heart to give their children what they need and to make them happy. They also know, however, that some goods cannot be given but must be developed and achieved in the child's own life. We cannot simply give our children the happiness that comes from finding a vocation, a spouse, or inner strength. Trying to give such goods would, in effect, subvert and undermine them. So too we have to ask whether there might be research aims that, however well intentioned, would seek to bestow traits of character and skill that have no value apart from the process whereby they are developed and achieved. We are, that is, forced to ask hard questions about projects aimed at "enhancing" human nature.

Where do such ambivalent reflections lead? Bioethics directs our attention to *Bios*—to human bodily life in all its vulnerability and with all the goods (biological, rational, cultural, spiritual) that characterize it. For that life we seek health, and in that life we seek to avoid suffering. These are great goods of bodily life, but they sometimes compete with other, equally human goods. Relief of suffering is surely of great importance; yet it remains only one desideratum of a truly human life. At a few times and places it may seem imperative; at many times and places it is desirable; in a few times and places, because we judge other, competing goods to be even more fundamental to human life, it may be neither imperative nor desirable.

FINALLY . . .

Many of the threads of this discussion come together in one of the most famous passages in Dante's *Divine Comedy*. In Canto XXVI of the *Inferno*, with Vergil still his guide, Dante encounters the "false counselors," those who had used their gift of great intellect in ways that ultimately led others astray. Here it is that Dante meets Ulysses (Odysseus) and hears his story. In a passage that Dorothy Sayers called "perhaps the most beautiful thing in the whole *Inferno*," a passage that is evidently Dante's own invention and is certainly found neither in Homer nor in Vergil, Dante describes the last voyage of Ulysses.

Ulysses has made it safely home from years of wandering after the Trojan Wars. He has returned to his home—and to Ithaca, which he is to rule. But, in this invention of Dante's, he does not remain there. Even love for his son, his father, or his faithful wife Penelope cannot, he says, "conquer in me the restless itch to rove," to press beyond the boundaries of what is known. And so, Ulysses gathers together a crew to set sail once more. They reach the very boundary of the inhabited world as they know it, and Ulysses urges his shipmates on, arguing that men were made to move beyond what is already known. They forge ahead, only to sail into a storm that whirls the ship around three times, then lifts the poop deck high and plunges the prow down into the water. "And over our heads the hollow seas closed up."

When we remember that Ulysses is in hell, that as a false counselor he has used his great intellect to lead others astray, the point of the passage might seem clear. As a warning to Dante's readers it depicts, in the words of John Sinclair, "an eternal and insatiable human hunger and quest after knowledge of the world." The restless desire to know without limit, the will to sail uncharted waters, disastrously overcomes even the deepest loyalties of our finite life: to home, to father, to wife, to son. The passage is, I said, a warning; yet, Sinclair immediately adds, "and as we read it we forget the sin in contemplation of the sinner's greatness."

It is evidently one of the puzzles Dante scholars face: that Ulysses's proud and dignified description of his last voyage, a tale told by one who is quite literally damned, should have been made so enticing and compelling an account of the human need "to follow after knowledge and excellence." But that, perhaps, is the truth we have to ponder. Our finitude and freedom are not easily reconciled. The goods of life compete with each other, and if we do evil it may be done with great dignity and appeal—done even in the service of some good. The wisdom bioethics seeks is the wisdom to discern right order among such competing goods.

BIBLIOGRAPHY

Brown, Peter. *Augustine of Hippo*. New ed., with epilogue. Berkeley: University of California Press, 2000.

Jonas, Hans. "Philosophical Reflections on Experimenting with Human Subjects." In *Philosophical Essays: From Ancient Creed to Technological Man*, 105–31. Englewood Cliffs, NJ: Prentice-Hall, 1974.

Kinnell, Galway. "After Making Love We Hear Footsteps." In *Mortal Acts, Mortal Words*, 5. Boston: Houghton Mifflin, 1980.

Lewis, C. S. *The Abolition of Man*. New York: Macmillan, 1947.

Midgley, Mary. "Biotechnology and Monstrosity." *The Hastings Center Report* 30 (2000) 7–15.

Thomas, Lewis. *The Medusa and the Snail*. New York: Viking, 1979.

2

Bioethics in Public

Reflections on an Experience[1]

From January 16, 2002, to June 11, 2009, I served on the President's Council on Bioethics. Chaired first by Leon Kass (2001–2005) and then by Edmund Pellegrino (2005–2009), the Council met thirty-six times. Of its original eighteen members, nine served throughout the life of the Council. When asked, as I often was, whether I enjoyed the experience, my standard answer was, "It depends on what day you ask me."

One thing, however, seems clear to me: The Council, both because of the way it was constituted and the way it did its work, altered, at least for a time, the character of public bioethics. As the sociologist John H. Evans noted some years ago of debates about genetic engineering, the work of national bioethics commissions beginning in the mid-1970s changed in an important way. Attention shifted from a bioethics focused on the ends or goals that it was right to pursue to a bioethics in which certain ends were largely assumed

1. An earlier version of this essay appeared in *The New Atlantis* 26 (Fall 2009–Winter 2010). Reports of the President's Council on Bioethics—as well as transcripts of its meetings and background papers—are available online at https://bioethicsarchive.georgetown.edu/pcbe/index.html.

and debate focused on what means would best realize those ends. This much, of course, almost any observer might have noticed. What gave bite to Evans's work, however, was his well-documented argument that this shift was not an inevitable result of an increasingly pluralistic society. On the contrary, it was deliberate. It was aimed at protecting scientific research from public oversight, accomplishing this by vesting responsibility for such oversight not in legislative bodies elected by the public but in advisory commissions whose members were themselves active in the field of bioethics.

That approach was altered by the President's Council. As Leon Kass often noted, it was a Council "on" bioethics, not a Council "of" bioethicists. Its members brought very different sorts of expertise to the Council's work. Moreover, especially when it was (at least in my view) at its best, the Council listened to and talked with people who were knowledgeable experts about whatever issue was under discussion—and then did its own ethical reflection. The Council did not, at its best, simply ask others to do the ethical thinking for it.

This can be hard to do. It requires a serious willingness to try to understand those whose training and expertise are very different from one's own. It makes agreement a relatively rare achievement. Indeed, precisely by returning to a focus not just on means but also on the ends or goals of biotechnological advance, the Council almost guaranteed that consensus would not be its chief priority. Instead, exploring and examining competing goals became the primary task. Such exploration is unlikely to result in a large number of policy recommendations, but that is not its aim. The aim, rather, is to help the public and its elected representatives think about the implications of biotechnological advance for human life.

My own reflections here will focus on the critical response to the formation and beginning of the Council, the stem cell issue that dominated its initial meetings, work that took the Council in some respects beyond that initial issue and exemplified its approach to public bioethics, and the problems and possibilities of a public bioethics that is truly open to competing understandings of our humanity.

BEGINNINGS

The Council met for the first time on January 17–18, 2002. In his televised speech of August 9, 2001 (a date that took on special significance because of the pivotal role it played in his administration's policy regarding federal funding of embryonic stem cell research), President George W. Bush had announced his intention to form such a Council and had named Leon Kass to chair it. As it turned out, however, the events of September 11 delayed the formation of the Council and the beginning of its work until January 2002.

Although the formation of the Council was directly linked to controversies about embryonic stem cell research, and although the Council was specifically charged to monitor such research in relation to the administration's funding policy, its mandate was far more extensive. The Council was authorized "to undertake fundamental inquiry into the human and moral significance of developments in biomedical and behavioral science and technology" and asked "to develop a deep and comprehensive understanding of the issues that it considers." In pursuit of such goals, the Council was specifically freed from the need "to reach a single consensus position" on the issues it took up.

From the very beginning, however, there were critics who—notwithstanding the executive order's instruction that the Council "be guided by the need to articulate fully the complex and often competing moral positions" on the issues it studied—were confident that Council membership had been heavily stacked with opponents of embryonic stem cell research and who doubted the usefulness of the kind of bioethical inquiry that characterized the Council's approach. It is worth sampling a few of the earliest critical comments.

In an article published in *The Washington Post* on the day of the Council's first meeting (when its membership had just been announced), science writer Rick Weiss outlined the expectations shared by many. "Some observers say the president's council is politically stacked," Weiss noted, and, he observed, "the council's membership includes several well-known scholars with conservative leanings." Strangely, however, in mentioning such "conservative voices" on the Council, Weiss characterized Robert George—a well-known professor in Princeton's Department of Politics—as a "theologian" and failed to note that James Q. Wilson—though known, to be sure, as a political neoconservative—had defended human cloning in print. Francis Fukuyama was listed among the conservative voices on the Council and Rebecca Dresser among those who "carry more liberal credentials"; yet, an observer of the Council's deliberations on cloning and stem cell research would surely conclude that their views were very similar. Neither was opposed in principle to using cloned embryos for research, but each concluded that more time for public deliberation and for the establishment of a regulatory apparatus was needed before such research should proceed.

Even more striking perhaps was the concern—front and center in Weiss's article—that the work of the Council would be taken over by religious fundamentalists (a term Weiss did not trouble himself to define in any way). Quite near the beginning of the article, Weiss first made the connection.

> In November [of 2001], researchers announced that they had made the first human embryo clones, giving immediacy to warnings by religious conservatives and others that science is no longer serving the nation's moral will. At the same time, the United States was fighting a war to free a faraway nation from the grip of religious conservatives who were denounced for imposing their moral code on others.

The implication was unmistakable: While United States military forces were fighting against religious thinkers who wanted to impose their moral views on others, the President's Council might be in service of homegrown religious conservatives equally eager to impose their moral views in domestic politics. Lest anyone should miss the point, Weiss later cited "experts" who suggested that, were the Council to argue that "human embryos are inherently deserving of protection," it "could legitimize an effort to codify fundamentalist views into law." Evidently there were no grounds other than such (still undefined) fundamentalist ones on the basis of which one might oppose research that destroys embryos.

Equally noteworthy was Arthur Caplan's MSNBC column of January 17 characterizing the newly appointed body as "a council of clones"— that is, clones of Leon Kass, with respect to their views—"stacked with members who lean to the political right" and who "will rely on religious rather than secular principles" in their bioethical deliberations. The notion, mentioned by both Weiss and Caplan, that the Council's membership was stacked, proved to be rather far from the mark. Even apart from that simple matter of fact, however, other unspoken and unargued assumptions of Caplan's commentary are worth noting. An unwary reader might suppose that previous national bioethics bodies had been characterized by a wide spectrum of opinion on disputed matters, whereas in truth none ever had the deep divisions that the President's Council displayed in its deliberations about cloning embryos for research. An unwary reader might also suppose that the question of how religious beliefs ought to (or, evidently in Caplan's view, ought not to) enter into public debate was a settled question, whereas in truth it continues to be a topic on which philosophers, political theorists, and public intellectuals hold a variety of different positions.

It should have been possible for someone quite skeptical of directions the Council was likely to take to offer a more nuanced analysis of its membership—as an early piece by Ronald Bailey demonstrates. Writing in "reasononline" Bailey analyzed what he could find of the views and writings of Council members, offering "educated guesses" about their positions on three related issues: embryonic stem cell research, therapeutic cloning (as it was then called), and reproductive cloning (as it was then called). His predictions—that the Council would be at least 16–2 against reproductive cloning, 10–8 against therapeutic cloning, and split 9–9 on embryonic stem cell research—while not completely accurate, were remarkably prescient. Bailey, of course, would not ordinarily be characterized as a bioethicist. Perhaps a certain critical distance, freed from any sense that it would have been better had he himself been a Council member, accounts at least partially for the accuracy of his assessment.

There were, to be sure, knowledgeable bioethicists who did not fully accept characterizations of the Council such as those given by Weiss and Caplan. Thus, for example, Stuart Youngner noted that one could reasonably argue that the Council's membership reflected more diverse professional backgrounds than had been the case with previous national bioethics bodies. Nevertheless, other voices were louder and, in some cases—such as Glenn McGee's attacks on Leon Kass in the pages of the *American Journal of Bioethics* and its blog—so mean-spirited and petty that one could scarcely account for them on intellectual or academic grounds.

Even years later, after the Council had completed its work and the record should have been clear, a commentator such as Cathleen Kaveny, writing in *Commonweal*, could continue to characterize the Council as monochromatic—or, to the degree that it was diverse, as divided simply between "secular liberals" and "religious conservatives" (a characterization that cannot withstand serious examination).

The criticism that relatively few members of the Council had made their academic reputations as "bioethicists" is one that was made repeatedly as the Council did its work. The point of such an observation is generally to note that politics and political convictions, rather than the presumably disinterested thinking of academic bioethicists, had been allowed to hijack debate about important issues. But this raises—and begs—large questions about how public bioethics should be done.

The Council began its work focusing on debates surrounding the use (and destruction) of human embryos in research. Among the questions this raises is, of course, that of the status of human embryos and their place within the human community. Fundamental to our public arguments here has been a question of membership within the community and entitlement to its protection. Surely that is—and is properly—a political question. Whose good counts in the common good? Anyone who wants to pretend that this is a question for bioethics but not for politics needs to think longer and more carefully about the nature of political argument. Moreover, any notion that those who engage professionally in academic bioethics come free of normative commitments, able to adjudicate conflicting views without themselves being parties to the conflict, is unlikely to persuade many people who have been paying attention.

Thus, for example, in February 2006 Arthur Caplan, at that time Director of the University of Pennsylvania Center for Bioethics, emailed "friends" of the Center to detail ways in which the Center was "playing a key role in insuring that ideology does not overwhelm sound science." He listed a number of occasions when the Center's faculty had advised, among others, "policy makers." Their efforts, he suggested, were increasing the chances that elected officials "will support potentially life-saving [embryonic stem cell] research." None of this is surprising or illegitimate in an appeal for support, of course, but it stands in some tension with a claim that others have "politicized" bioethics. As I noted at the outset of this essay, the extensive social science research of John H. Evans has detailed ways in which the early development of bioethics in this country was intended to protect scientific research from public oversight. And more recently the philosopher George Khushf, after surveying extensively several controversies in bioethics, has suggested that when the interests of researchers are at stake, "they use the social status of their expertise to advance an ideology that works against a liberal exchange of ideas." This is quite a different reading of the facts than Caplan's suggestion that bioethicists are "insuring that ideology does not overwhelm sound science."

One more early response to the Council is worth noting, for it reveals a certain mindset. The Council devoted an entire session—the second session of its very first meeting—to a discussion of Nathaniel Hawthorne's short story "The Birth-Mark." Commenting on this session in *The New Yorker*—in a short "Talk of the Town" piece titled "Science Fiction"—Jerome Groopman characterized this as beginning "not with facts but with fiction." Is it not puzzling to find Groopman expressing the desire that our policy on stem cell research be "based on fact, not on literature or aesthetics"? There is, of course, a serious point here that might be argued (though Groopman only asserts and does not trouble himself to argue). One might argue that there is no bioethical wisdom to be gained through the study of literature. I think such a view would be mistaken, but it could certainly be put forward with serious arguments. What is very strange, however, is that this view should be given expression in the pages of *The New Yorker*, perhaps our most well-known literary magazine—which can only leave one to wonder what might have moved Groopman to make this sort of criticism or *The New Yorker* to print it.

STEM CELLS

The speech of President Bush on August 9, 2001, in which he announced his intention to establish the President's Council on Bioethics, was not primarily about the Council. It was about stem cell research—or, more precisely, about whether and to what degree the federal government should provide funding to support such research. The issue was not the morality, legality, or even wisdom of stem cell research, which was not prohibited by law and could be funded privately. At stake was simply the administration's policy with respect to federally funded research that could not be undertaken without the destruction of human embryos.

Thinking—and arguing—about that policy, however, immersed the Council in the subject of human cloning and the meaning of human embryonic life, matters that continued to haunt the Council throughout its tenure. Well before the Council came into existence, Congress had already prohibited (through what was known as the Dickey Amendment, first enacted in 1995) the use of federal funds to support research that destroyed human embryos. With the announcement in 1997 of the cloning of the lamb Dolly, the question of embryo-destructive research suddenly was intertwined with the seeming possibility of human cloning. For one way—indeed, in certain important respects, the preferred way—to get embryos for research is to clone them.

In any case, the intertwining of these issues meant that the focus of debates about cloning had shifted. In the immediate aftermath of the Dolly announcement, the question "Shall we clone?" had been taken to mean: Shall we try to produce through gestation and live birth a cloned human being (in the way a sheep had been cloned to produce Dolly)? To that question many people answered no. Without necessarily being able fully to articulate their reasons, many turned against the very idea of such cloning.

From the perspective of researchers, however, this provided an occasion to reopen the question of funding for embryo-destructive research. To the question, "Shall we clone?" they replied, "Certainly not." By that, however, they meant only, "We should not clone a human embryo, implant and gestate it, and bring it to live birth." But, they suggested, we should be able to clone embryos for use in research, as long as those embryos were not implanted, gestated, or brought to live birth. That is, some in the research and bioethics communities used the occasion of Dolly's birth to reopen the question that Congress had tried to close with respect to federal funding of embryo-destructive research. Indeed, it was precisely cloned embryos that were of most interest to researchers because of their potential for producing exactly the disease models researchers wanted to study.

This gave rise to the linguistic distinction between "therapeutic" and "reproductive" cloning, a distinction that eventually proved unsatisfactory to both its defenders and its critics. For those of us who were critics of the language it seemed to confuse rather than clarify the issue. If, for example, one believes that an embryo is a human being in its earliest stage of development, then all cloning is reproductive. Moreover, to call research cloning therapeutic was deceptive in several ways. The research was unlikely to be therapeutic for anyone for quite some time, if ever, and it was, of course, just the opposite of therapeutic for the embryos that would be produced, used, and, in the process, destroyed.

Proponents of the language also discovered that it did not serve their purposes as well as they might have hoped. Their hope had been that negative reverberations (in the public mind) of the term *cloning* would be overcome by the positive tone of the word *therapeutic*. This did not prove to be the case, and proponents soon switched from talk of "therapeutic cloning" to the more technical "somatic cell nuclear transfer." Thus, for example, in 2002 the National Academy of Sciences released a report titled "Scientific and Medical Aspects of Human Reproductive Cloning." Characterizing human reproductive cloning as "an assisted reproductive technology that would be carried out with the goal of creating a human being," the report then pivoted terminologically: "There is a very different procedure, here termed nuclear transplantation to produce stem cells—but variously called nonreproductive cloning, therapeutic cloning, research cloning, or somatic cell nuclear transfer (SCNT) to produce stem cells—whose aim is the creation of embry-onic stem (ES) cells for clinical and research purposes."

The attempt to sanitize the act of reproductive cloning by labeling it a "very different procedure" called nuclear transplantation to produce stem cells was a misstep from the outset. Whether the aim is to engage in research or to produce a child, the initial act and the product of that act are the same. The difference—whether to implant and gestate the embryo produced by that initial act—is a further matter of will and choice, depend-ing on the purposes we have in mind. Both what was called reproductive cloning and that purportedly "very different procedure" called somatic cell nuclear transfer begin by doing the same thing—producing an embryo, whether for use in assisted reproduction or for use in research aimed at developing therapies for the suffering.

Perhaps it is no surprise that the Council spent almost an entire hour-and-a-half session debating terminology—talking not about cloning but about what language to use when talking about cloning. This was, in my view, time well spent, and there are lessons to be learned from it. One of the most useful things a body such as the Council can do is seek clarity in ways that may benefit public deliberation and debate more generally. In July 2002, the Council released its first report, *Human Cloning and Human Dignity*. Chapter 3 of the report is titled simply "On Terminology" and contains a long discussion of the terminological tangles into which a lack of clarity can lead us. This chapter's discussion was not a surreptitious attempt to choose terminology that would, in effect, decide the matter in favor of one view. Its aim was to sort out the terminological puzzles that often got in the way of shared understanding and clear disagreement.

Probably no terminology can do perfectly everything we want it to accomplish. But the Council, looking for a way to recognize both that the initial act remains the same (whatever our purposes) but also that the purposes make a difference in our overall moral judgment, finally chose to distinguish between "cloning-to-produce-children" and "cloning-for-biomedical-research." All of this was, as I have noted, simply prolegomenon to the central moral debate about how to evaluate morally cloning-for-bio-medical-research. On that issue, contrary to many of the early predictions by detractors, the Council was deeply divided, though hardly along a fault line separating religious conservatives from secular liberals. Chapter 6 of the report incarnated that divide, making, as best the Council was able, the moral case both for and against cloning-for-biomedical-research.

That chapter, together with the chapter on terminology, constitute, I think, lasting contributions of the Council and evidence that its approach can enrich public awareness and understanding. On the actual policy question itself, the deep divisions were apparent. Ten members of the Council supported a moratorium on cloning-for-biomedical-research, and seven favored moving ahead with such research, though only after regulatory controls were in place. (One of the original eighteen members had resigned—and not yet been replaced—before the report was released.) It was, however, possible for everyone to claim a victory, if such claims matter. Because three of the ten-person majority favored a moratorium but not a permanent ban on cloning-for-biomedical-research, its advocates could—and did—emphasize that a majority of the Council opposed a ban.

One other element of the Council's approach was clearly evident in this first report. All members were offered the opportunity to append "personal statements" to the report, and fourteen elected to do so. The executive order establishing the Council had charged it "to develop a deep and comprehensive understanding of the issues that it considers" and had freed it of any need "to reach a single consensus position" on those issues. In the first instance, therefore, the Council's role was not policymaking but educative, aimed less at solving than at unpacking the complexities posed by advances in biotechnology. Therefore, chapter 6 explored in detail—and made as good a case as we were able—for *each* of the opposed positions on cloning-for-biomedical-research. Not content with that display of differences, many Council members chose to append personal statements, providing their own view on one or another aspect of the issue.

This is very far from attempting to tell elected officials what they ought to decide. Perhaps it may seem to some to be too chaotic, almost a *reductio ad absurdum* of the decision to eschew methods aimed primarily at achieving consensus. But it is also enriching in many ways, and *Human Cloning and Human Dignity* continues to provide a useful illustration of a way to do public bioethics that captures some of its richness and seeks to develop the rare ability actually to understand a disagreement.

BEYOND STEM CELLS

The Council's term (having been renewed several times) was to expire on September 30, 2009. But on June 10, 2009, Council members received letters from the White House informing them that their service on the

Council would end the following day. In an article in the *New York Times* an administration press officer was quoted as saying that the Council had been "a philosophically leaning advisory group" rather than (what was evidently now desired) one offering "practical policy options."

This was not an entirely accurate assessment. *Human Cloning and Human Dignity* had, after all, set forth a (majority and minority) case for two different policy options. Likewise, *Reproduction & Responsibility* had concluded with a discussion of policy options and recommendations and even specific legislative measures. Nevertheless, it is surely true that the Council focused less on policy recommendations than on exploration of what is at stake in biotechnological advance. If there is loss in such an approach, there is also gain, as we can see by considering three additional Council reports: *Beyond Therapy, Alternative Sources of Human Pluripotent Stem Cells*, and *Controversies in the Determination of Death*. I will comment briefly on the second and third of these and in more detail on the first.

If I want to drive from Chicago to Indianapolis, the obvious route for most of the way is I-65. If, however, I'm told that I may not take that route, but I very much want to get to Indianapolis, I will look for alternatives. I will do my best to see whether there is not some other way to achieve my objective while still adhering to the instruction that puts I-65 off limits for my travel. In some respects, this is what the Bush administration policy with respect to federal funding of embryonic stem cell research did. It recognized the importance of the goal and, by placing one route to that goal largely off limits, encouraged researchers—and all of us—to think creatively about alternatives.

That kind of thinking is the point of a short Council report with the ungainly title *Alternative Sources of Human Pluripotent Stem Cells*. The Council began here with a commitment to two goods that had seemed incompatible in the stem cell debate: the advance of scientific research in order to better the human condition, and a defense of the dignity of every human life. Perhaps in some circumstances these are and must remain simply incompatible, but we should not ignore the possibility that the aims of research may be advanced in ways that do not violate the consciences of a significant number of American citizens.

To that end, *Alternative Sources* examined four proposals that had been advanced by serious thinkers—proposals for means by which pluripotent human stem cells (capable of doing almost anything that an embryonic stem cell can do) might be obtained without the destruction of embryos.

26

Here I will not discuss or examine the four proposals themselves, though it is worth noting that the fourth of them—what was called somatic cell dedifferentiation—is roughly the approach that later succeeded in producing induced pluripotent stem cells. The report examined all four methods, with an eye to considering both their scientific feasibility and their ethical acceptability. No policy proposals were offered; instead, the Council endorsed the proposals as "worthy of further public discussion" and encouraged their "scientific exploration in accordance with the preliminary ethical judgments" offered in the report.

Would it really have been better—of more use in public discussion—had the Council proposed a practical policy option rather than this examination of alternatives? If an attempt to satisfy several different, and possibly conflicting, concerns of citizens is itself a public good, then here is a model worth considering. It does more than simply take differing views into consideration. By waiting patiently and prescinding from hasty attempts at closure, it may find ways to do justice to the conscientious commitments of many citizens. There is, of course, no guarantee that this will or must happen, but *Alternative Sources* offers at least a hopeful illustration of what may sometimes be possible.

Controversies in the Determination of Death, released rather late in the Council's tenure and after Edmund Pellegrino had replaced Leon Kass as chairman, is a deeply philosophical exploration of the meaning of death—once again, with no policy prescriptions offered. This does not mean, however, that the report has no practical implications.

Physicians generally had determined death—and often still do—by observing the permanent loss of heart and lung activity. But for the last half century or so, the use of respirators has made possible continuation of cardiovascular activity even when all capacity for brain activity has been permanently lost. Hence, in both medicine and law there had developed increasing reliance on a neurological rather than a cardiovascular standard for determining death. A person who had suffered irreversible loss of all brain activity was deemed dead, even if mechanical ventilation meant that heart and lung activity was sustained in the corpse (which did not, therefore, look the way we expect a corpse to look). Many of the organs used for transplant have been taken from just such corpses, for the continued activity of heart and lungs means that the organs do not deteriorate but remain in a condition suitable for transplant. Indeed, without the newer neurological standard for determining death, there would surely be far fewer organs available for transplant.

The fact that thinking in terms of "brain death" increases the possibilities for transplantation is not itself, however, a sufficient reason to use the neurological standard. Moreover, the rationale for using it—namely, that a body that has suffered irreversible loss of all brain activity can no longer function as an integrated whole—had never been entirely persuasive and had increasingly been confronted with troubling counterexamples. This did not necessarily mean that the standard was mistaken, but it did mean that the understanding of death on which it depended needed examination and, perhaps, better formulation.

That is what *Controversies in the Determination of Death* seeks to do. Not to offer judgments about transplant policy. Not to suppose that the meaning of death is a purely empirical matter for medicine alone to contemplate. But, rather, to think again about what it means that an organism is living—and what, then, it means that an organism has died. Eventually, the Council concluded that the earlier rationale, which emphasized the necessity of brain activity for the body to function as an integrated whole, could not be sustained. In its place the Council offered a somewhat different—and, it must be said, more complicated—description of how any living organism works to sustain itself through an openness to its environment and an inner drive that moves it to engage with that environment. This happens most obviously for human beings through consciousness, but engagement with the world may take place even when one is unconscious but continues spontaneously to exhibit an inner drive to breathe and take in oxygen from the environment.

One might, of course, say that this leaves everything—with respect to policy—in place, and so, in a sense, it does. But the report acknowledges a deep philosophical puzzle in our current approach to transplantation, a puzzle that cannot in honesty be ignored. It thinks through that puzzle and offers a better—though perhaps more complex—way of thinking about what it means for human beings to live and to die. Perhaps it is good that our society should seek clarity about the meaning of death, even if that clarity asks us to do more than just continue transplanting organs in search of a few more years—even if it asks us to pause and think carefully about death, that most philosophical of subjects.

Of all the reports issued by the President's Council, perhaps none better exemplifies the manner in which the Council approached the task of public bioethics than *Beyond Therapy*. It bears the impress of some long-standing concerns of Leon Kass, the Council's first chairman, but not only his concerns. For example, Council member Michael Sandel, drawing extensively on much of the material developed in Council meetings, wrote first an article in *The Atlantic* and then a book, each titled "The Case against Perfection."

Surely, *Beyond Therapy* is not the sort of report we had come to expect from national bioethics commissions. Although it takes up several different issues, it is really one long, sustained, often philosophical argument that makes no policy recommendations at all. I sometimes thought that the report might better be titled "'Toward Perfection," for it is about what it means to be the sort of beings we are, with the limits inherent in our humanity, but also with limitless aspirations to surpass those boundaries in various ways.

Nor is surpassing them always or necessarily a bad thing. When, seeking to better our lives, we use our freedom—which is also a central characteristic of our humanity—to transcend limits that once seemed simply given, often we accomplish much that is good. But, of course, there may be limits that ought not to be surpassed—sorrows that it is good to experience, bodily decline that is built into the trajectory of a truly human life, a child we have been given rather than the child we might have hoped to fashion.

We can become inhuman in either of two ways—by acting in a manner that is less than human or by striving to be more than human. In *Human Cloning and Human Dignity* the Council had turned its attention to action that would be less than human in our treatment of the weakest and most vulnerable among us. In *Beyond Therapy* attention shifted to the temptation to be more than human in the pursuit of our limitless desire for perfection.

The heart of the report lies in chapters 2 through 5, which treat successively the topics of better children, superior performance, ageless bodies, and happy souls. It is noteworthy, however, that the report is not organized around the standard issues of eugenics, enhancement, and the uses of technology. On the contrary, it is organized around common, perfectly understandable, and (in many respects) quite appropriate human desires—for healthy and successful children, for excellent performance in the tasks we undertake, for more years of life and more life in the years we have, and for the sort of flourishing that comes from inner peace. In service of these almost limitless desires, we may make use of a wide array of different technologies.

We can select the sex, perhaps even some traits, of our children and use drugs to enhance their attention and regulate their behavior. We can look upon our bodies as simply another piece of equipment to be improved in ways that are not really self-involving. In the quest to find ways to retard aging, we can easily confuse (quantitatively) more of this life with the (qualitatively) different life that our hearts truly desire. We can use drugs that blunt memories or that enhance mood to medicalize much of life.

A reader of *Beyond Therapy* may begin to see the folly of depicting the Council's work as perpetuation of the culture wars by other means. If those on the right characteristically fear that biotechnological advances may undermine the natural order, and those on the left characteristically fear that biotechnological advances are the product of a market mentality that reduces every human good to a commodity, how shall we pigeonhole *Beyond Therapy*—in which both sorts of concerns are manifestly present? Both are present because *Beyond Therapy* is not a policy primer but an invitation to reflect on where we are going, before we simply arrive and are surprised to find that our destination was unanticipated and is now troubling.

Helping us to think about such questions is the true contribution of *Beyond Therapy*. Indeed, policy recommendations, eschewed by the report, might, by focusing attention on themselves, have undermined the invitation to reflection. But there is also, I think, a deeper reason why the report offers no recommendations. The problem *Beyond Therapy* explores—our limitless desires and our aspiration to be, perhaps, more than human—is not the sort of problem a policy can solve. Of course, thinking more clearly and carefully will also not solve that problem; hence, there are limits to what the report itself can hope to accomplish. The problem, and any "solution," go much deeper. We should, therefore, turn to *Beyond Therapy* not as a solution to the problem of limitless desire but, rather, as an invitation to think together about what it means to be human. In so doing, we may come not only to understand but also to honor and appreciate some of the limits that characterize our humanity.

PROBLEMS AND POSSIBILITIES

Doing bioethics in public, in the way the President's Council attempted it, brings with it certain risks and problems. When we seek not a lowest-common-denominator policy but, instead, discussion of morally complex questions by people who bring to that discussion very different normative commitments, those who are unwilling to enter into a discussion not guaranteed to culminate in a policy proposal, or those made uneasy by the kind of give-and-take such argument entails, may be dissatisfied.

In 2002, during some of the work preparatory to the writing of *Beyond Therapy*, the Council heard from various experts about research into pharmacological means of enhancing memory and blunting traumatic memories. Dr. James McGaugh, Director of the Center for Neurobiology of Learning and Memory at the University of California at Irvine, spoke at length to the Council about the possibility of relieving post-traumatic stress disorder through drugs that hinder the consolidation of memories. In the conversation that followed his presentation, Dr. McGaugh on several occasions recognized that, although there are obvious benefits to relieving strong memories of remembered trauma, there may also be reasons why we should remember trauma. That is a "judgment call," or a "trade-off question," he noted at several points in the conversation.

Ironically, however, Dr. McGaugh's own memory of the session seems to have been blunted. After the Council had, in *Beyond Therapy*, developed some of those reasons why we might hesitate simply to give a drug (were it available) to weaken traumatic memories, he recalled his presentation and commented, "They didn't say anything at the time but later they went ballistic on it." Anyone interested might look at section II ("Memory and Happiness") of chapter 5 of *Beyond Therapy*. My own view is that, if this is what Dr. McGaugh calls going "ballistic," he has spent insufficient time in conversations in which people reflect critically on normative questions. A society eager to forge ahead with publicly supported pharmacological research must also ask itself—in advance—some of the questions that chapter raises. Does memory-blunting risk falsifying our perception of the world? Does it risk making us too comfortable with some of the terrible things that happen in our world? Does a truthful identity seek to integrate rather than edit out the pain and unhappiness of life? Even while stating that there is "little doubt" that some memories are so painful and intrusive that the impulse to relieve them is "fully understandable," the Council also invited the American public to think prospectively rather than only retrospectively about the moral significance of memory and research into pharmacological means of blunting it. That is, the Council thought of the task of public bioethics not as protecting scientific research from oversight but as enriching public deliberation about the place of research in our common life together.

If researchers do not always appreciate this, neither do bioethicists. Locked into a particular angle of vision, they may be disturbed to find in the Council's approach what Ruth Macklin called "sharp differences from those found in books and articles by mainstream bioethicists." She criticized the use of "poetic and metaphoric language" in place of "empirical evidence and reasoned arguments." To take an example dear to my own heart, Macklin criticized an essay of my own, in which I used a poem to help illustrate what it means to speak of a child as a "gift." Such language, however, is hardly intended to eliminate reasoned argument; on the contrary, without it we are unable to explore the full meaning and significance of procreation as a human activity—in order then to go on and argue about it. Thus, describing children as "gifts" does not make the description true, but it offers a way of thinking that can be discussed and examined as we seek to learn the truth.

Macklin's objection goes deeper, however. She seems to believe that to speak of a child as a gift is inescapably religious language and, as such, can only be a "conversation stopper" in gatherings that are not themselves explicitly religious. I'm not certain what I think of the first of these two claims. It may be that, plumbed to its depths, characterizing children as gifts is intelligible only in the context of religious belief. It may be—but not all agree. Michael Sandel observes, reasonably enough, that "we commonly speak of an athlete's gift, or a musician's, without making any assumption about whether or not the gift comes from God. What we mean is simply that the talent in question is not wholly the athlete's or the musician's own doing; whether he has nature, fortune, or God to thank for it, the talent is an endowment that exceeds his control."

But it is Macklin's second claim that is the more important. Let us suppose that speaking of children as gifts does, when fully explicated, draw upon the language of religion. Why need such talk be ruled out of public bioethical discussion? Why need it be a conversation stopper when not all share those beliefs? Though Macklin no doubt sincerely thinks that her views are based solely on "empirical evidence and reasoned argument," one seldom has to press very hard on such views to find in them a buried metaphysic (as, for example, the language of autonomy implies). All angles of vision, including purportedly empirical ones, are theory-laden from the outset. We can make our language less interesting, but not less metaphorical.

Moreover, language that draws on a wide array of humanistic perspectives does several important things. It challenges us to ponder whether a world in which we had no sense of our own and others' "giftedness" would really be a better world. It undergirds, as Sandel notes, a certain humility about our possibilities, it suggests limits to human responsibility, and it encourages us to think of ourselves in solidarity with those less fortunate. But it does more than challenge us. It also offers to enlarge our vision of what it means to be human. It is precisely the function of imaginative language to uncover meanings we might otherwise overlook.

If this language often has its roots in religious thought, then our public deliberations about bioethics need to be open to such thought. Those deliberations would be impoverished were we to suppose that moral reasoning demands that we all set aside the most personally distinctive features of how we understand the world. What we owe each other, on the contrary, is precisely the best reasons we can produce, whether they prove to be personally distinctive or not. Acknowledging this will help to keep us from falling into the trap of supposing that debate about a matter such as embryo research is a merely scientific question. It is not. It is about the nature of human life and about the role and limits of scientific research.

In his *Leviathan* Thomas Hobbes observed that "the doctrine of right and wrong is perpetually disputed, both by the pen and the sword; whereas the doctrine of lines and figures, is not so." Why? Why, Hobbes asks, do we constantly dispute about moral matters but not about mathematics or science? Because, he suggests, in matters mathematical and scientific our interests are seldom involved and truth is "a thing that crosses no man's ambition, profit, or lust." Suppose, however, that our interests were on one occasion or another involved, that we had a stake in the truth of some mathematical or scientific dispute, then, Hobbes suggests, we would treat science as we do morality. "For I doubt not, but if it had been a thing contrary to any man's right of dominion, or to the interest of men that have dominion, that the three angles of a triangle, should be equal to two angles of a square; that doctrine should have been, if not disputed, yet by the burning of all books of geometry, suppressed, as far as he whom it concerned was able." We need not be quite as suspicious as Hobbes to see that, in many of the important bioethical debates, "interests" and agendas of various sorts are involved—and involved on every side of the arguments.

The desire to fix in advance the limits of acceptable argument manifests a kind of nervousness and anxiety about democratic discourse, which almost always—and certainly when important matters are at stake—involves a conflict of visions and wills. That is the very stuff of a shared moral life, and a claim to the contrary is unworthy of public deliberation in a great nation. A body such as the President's Council, enjoined to eschew consensus and to think through and articulate our disagreements, can make a contribution to our public deliberations very different from what is contributed by a consensus (and, very probably, lowest-common-denominator) policy recommendation. The latter invites only acceptance or rejection; it does not inspire to fresh or more expansive reflection, nor does it open up much space for those who would speak out of very different normative traditions.

Among those different traditions will, of course, be religious angles of vision. There is no reason to exclude them from the conversation. To be sure, when as a Christian I enter into such conversation, I do not speak merely on behalf of a particular religious interest group. Rather, beginning from a particular standpoint, I seek to learn and articulate an understanding of what is, quite simply, human. An epistemologically particular starting point may be a place from which to see what is ontologically universal. We all begin from such particular standpoints. That is not problematic; it is the human condition. What is problematic is a failure to acknowledge that we do so.

We all have a stake therefore in how public bioethical debate is structured. Indeed, it may be that we should care more about how it is structured than about what is decided on any given occasion. The conversation and the arguments never reach a definitive end. But a public conversation that leaves policymaking to elected officials, who can be held accountable, and that is designed to focus not just on means but also on the ends or goals of biotechnological advance—a conversation, that is, about matters on which one can safely predict we are not all likely to agree—provides all citizens an opportunity to reflect upon who we are as a people and how we may best structure our common life on matters of great moral significance.

BIBLIOGRAPHY

Evans, John H. *Playing God? Human Genetic Engineering and the Rationalization of Public Bioethical Debate.* Chicago: University of Chicago Press, 2002.

Khushf, George. "Owning Up to Our Agendas: On the Role and Limits of Science in Debates about Embryos and Brain Death." *Journal of Law, Medicine and Ethics* 34 (2006) 58–76.

Macklin, Ruth. "Dignity Is a Useless Concept: It Means No More than Respect for Persons or Their Autonomy." *British Medical Journal* 327 (2003) 1419–20.

Sandel, Michael J. *The Case against Perfection: Ethics in the Age of Genetic Engineering.* Cambridge: Belknap Press of Harvard University Press, 2007.

3

Biotech Enhancement and the History of Redemption[1]

In 2003 the President's Council on Bioethics released a report titled *Beyond Therapy: Biotechnology and the Pursuit of Happiness.* It is, I think, a very striking document—both in its own right as an exploration of its topic, and also as a government document that is highly philosophical in character and entirely without any policy recommendations. As one who participated in the discussions that led to the writing of *Beyond Therapy*, I both recognize its peculiar character and believe that it made a distinctive contribution to thought about human enhancement.

In April 2004, Michael Sandel, who was also a Council member, published an article in *The Atlantic* titled "The Case against Perfection." In slightly expanded form that article became a book under the same title, published in 2007. Sandel's illustrations and examples are drawn almost entirely from the Council's meetings, although the *Atlantic* article nowhere notes that. There is a passing reference to this in the later book, when Sandel makes clear how his own preferred analysis differs from that of *Beyond Therapy*—a difference I will in due course take up.

Each of these analyses, different though they are in important respects, offers reasons why we should be hesitant to endorse genetic and

1. An earlier version of this essay appeared in *The New Atlantis* 45 (Spring 2015).

pharmacological enhancement. Neither argument necessarily calls for rejection of any and every technique of enhancement, but the concerns raised by both arguments give serious reasons for hesitation, and I will work my way through them in some detail.

What I have in mind, however, goes a little beyond what either *Beyond Therapy* or *The Case against Perfection* does. I want to use them as a starting point for trying to think theologically about enhancement. This is not quite the same as what gets called posthumanism or transhumanism; for, after all, Christian hope focuses not on the overcoming or obliteration of our humanity but on its fulfillment.

My goal is not so much to render judgment on one or another possible technique for enhancement, nor even to sort through the thorny problem of distinguishing therapy from enhancement, but instead to place the problem within a theological framework, which is, I think, both useful in some ways and complicating in other ways. Useful because the reasons for hesitation offered by the Council and by Sandel give us a way to pour content into certain theological affirmations. Complicating because the complete story of God's action in Christ to redeem the world points us toward a future that does something more than just endorse the concerns articulated by *Beyond Therapy* and *The Case against Perfection*.

The title of this essay—referring as it does to "the History of Redemption"—suggests the framework within which I am thinking. In the massive and never completed volumes of his *Church Dogmatics* Karl Barth envisions ethics as offering an account of human action that corresponds to the threefold form of God's action in creation, reconciliation, and redemption. Because we are God's creatures, there must be some account that accepts, honors, and celebrates distinctively human agency. Because we are sinners whom God has in Jesus acted to reconcile, our life is disordered in countless ways, not least in our search for mastery and self-sufficiency. And because we are heirs of the future God has promised, we will one day be perfected—really enhanced—in a way that does not obliterate our created humanity but, rather, expresses God's faithfulness to it. I want to borrow not the substance but the structure of Barth's account, using it as an approach for thinking about enhancement.

Without attempting in any way to do justice to the richness of Barth's lavishly developed structure, I simply suggest that Christian moral reflection on almost any important topic—in this case, enhancement—cannot ignore any of the three angles of vision that Barth distinguishes. The three

36

angles of vision do not simply follow one another in lockstep sequence, nor does any one ever replace another. But even if, as Barth himself noted, it is difficult to combine the three, it is still important, as he put it, to recall that in ethics our task is "to accompany this history of God and man from creation to reconciliation and redemption, indicating the mystery of the encounter at each point on the path according to its own distinctive character."

CREATED LIFE

Beyond Therapy discusses at length several different kinds of biotechnical enhancement—among them attempts to produce better children, ageless bodies, or happy souls. Each of those discussions is informative and thought-provoking, but I want to attend chiefly to the discussion (in chapter 3) of attempts to achieve superior performance. Perhaps this is not the most important or dangerous form of enhancement, but the discussion in this chapter has always seemed to me to be both profound and puzzling. And it invites us, I think, to theological reflection.

Most obviously in the world of competitive sports, but also in other realms of life, we look for ways to improve our performance. Some ways, such as exercise and nutrition, may seem relatively commonplace and unproblematic. Others, such as pharmacological or genetic measures to enhance our physical capacities, seem more far-reaching and are more likely to make us fear that there is something problematic about trying to be what Carl Elliott called "better than well."

Why should or might such enhancement techniques trouble us? *Beyond Therapy* notes and discusses a few standard concerns, only in the end to suggest that they do not penetrate to the central problem. They merit brief discussion, however, in order to fill out the reasons for concern.

One issue has to do with fairness. Perhaps enhancement could give a boost to those whom nature has not blessed with many talents or gifts, and that would seem like a good thing. We might wonder, though, whether the desired result would really come to pass. If opportunities for enhancement were available to relatively few, we might exacerbate rather than even out the inequalities already present in our native endowments. If, on the other hand, enhancements were available to all, differences in natural talents would still remain and greater equality would not necessarily result. So something more than a worry about fairness is needed to account for our unease.

Pressure to improve

It could also be that an undercurrent of coercion would manifest itself. We might feel pressure—either from within ourselves or from others—to find ways to improve our capacities. Such pressure might nudge us in directions we do not really want to go or trap us on an endless treadmill of ambition. Perhaps so. Still, as *Beyond Therapy* notes, many areas of life are already marked by pressure to perform well and succeed. Nor would we want it otherwise. Thus, for example, we look for and admire excellence in musical performance, and we would like the hands of our surgeon to be steady and skillful. Moreover, the fundamental problem cannot be simply that some of us might feel pressured to use enhancement techniques. If there were nothing problematic in itself about the techniques, we would hardly be worried about pressure to use them.

Yet another obvious concern is that in our eagerness to enhance our capacities we might turn to techniques whose safety was unproven and which turned out to be harmful. Clearly, this is a serious concern, worth taking seriously, although the relentless progress of modern research medicine needs to be set over against any such worry. Even apart from our confidence in medical advance, however, *Beyond Therapy* notes a question we might ask ourselves in some instances. Why should we not run certain risks in the pursuit of excellent performance? Professional athletes, for example, often accept risk of harm as a necessary aspect of their drive to succeed. Thus, in the midst of ongoing discussions about the danger to professional football players caused by concussions, Chris Conte, at the time a safety for the Chicago Bears, was quoted as saying, "I'd rather have the experience of playing in the NFL and die 10 to 15 years earlier than not play in the NFL and have a long life." Why exactly should we prefer a safe, well-balanced life to one that risks much in the pursuit of superior performance? After all, as *Beyond Therapy* notes, "all human excellence, to some degree, requires at least some distortion."

A deeper concern emerges, however, in the Council's suggestion that the character of our agency might be undermined by techniques of enhancement. Consider the difference between improving my skill as a hitter through improved training and practice or through the use of performance-enhancing drugs. When we train, the capacities we want to improve are improved precisely by using them. The changes (and, it is hoped, improvements) come then from "putting our bodies to work" rather than from having "our bodies 'worked on.'" This means, *Beyond Therapy* suggests, that our character as agents might be diminished by the use of enhancement techniques. We "become 'better' by no longer being fully ourselves."

Why should the use of enhancement diminish our agency in a way that increased and improved training does not? One possible reason, given some credence by the Council, is that, whereas improvement that comes through training is intelligible to the agent, improvement produced by some sort of biotechnical aid will seem from the agent's perspective to happen almost by magic. At least in part, then, the agent is alienated from his own activity. I don't think, however, that this can completely explain the idea of diminished agency. While there does seem to be a recognizable difference between working our body and having it worked upon, in both cases an agent might have some comprehension of the reasons for improved performance, and in neither case would an agent be likely to understand fully the connection between what is done and the improvement that results. So diminished agency must point to something more than just the fact that an agent might not himself understand his improved performance.

The concern of *Beyond Therapy* is not simply that our agency could be diminished but, rather, that we might undermine a specifically *human* form of agency—excellent activity in which, as much as is possible, the doer is fully and willingly invested in the deed. As *Beyond Therapy* puts it, "The runner on steroids or with genetically enhanced muscles is still, of course, a human being who runs. But the doer of the deed is, arguably, less obviously *himself* and less obviously *human* than his unaltered counterpart."

We could, as the document notes, program a computer to play chess at a very high level. Is it "doing" the same thing as its human opponent? It may produce a well-executed game of chess, but that does not necessarily make it a great chess player. Likewise, we do not want to treat ourselves "as if we were batting machines to be perfected." Or again, suppose we were able to produce what appeared to be moral excellences—courage, humility, concern for others—by using a pill that bypassed the agent's need for character development or training in virtue. Might not something distinctively human thereby be lost?

The concern then is not simply agency, but distinctively *human* agency and excellence. What does *Beyond Therapy* mean by this? I think it wants to point us to something that, while simple to state, gets at the complexity of our humanity. Near the beginning of the *Nicomachean Ethics*, as Aristotle considers what will fulfill a human being, he suggests that the answer lies in "whatever is his proper function" (or, more literally, "proper work"). That

distinctive function must go beyond what human beings share with plant life (nourishment and growth), and also beyond what they share with the other animals (sense perception, desire for what is perceived, and movement to secure what is desired). Distinctively human action is carried out in conjunction, Aristotle says, with "the rational element" of the self. At its highest and most excellent it is not merely instinctive.

Human activity is marked by reflective purposiveness. Hence, for human beings, unlike the other animals, there is no naturally given unity of doer and deed. Marked by a kind of inwardness and self-transcendence, we are both located in our bodies and dislocated from them by reflection and choice. To overcome that dislocation without ceasing to be reflecting and choosing animals is needed if we are to achieve the kind of wholeness in which the doer is fully invested in the deed. "At such moments [of wholeness] the athlete experiences and displays something like the unity of doer and deed one observes in other animals, but for humans that unity is a *notable achievement* which far transcends what mere animals are capable of." Thus, the problem with some techniques of enhancement, at least if *Beyond Therapy* is correct, is that they alienate us further from ourselves, exacerbating the self's division rather than unifying doer and deed. To use techniques that are calculated to bypass our own will and reflection is to lose something of the distinctively human character of our performance. The body is more like a horse being whipped by a rider than "a body gracefully and harmoniously at work." Put more theologically, perhaps we could say that something of the excellence that human beings are created to achieve and enact is undermined, diminished, or lost.

To be sure, when we turn to enhancement as a means to superior performance, we do so as willful, choosing human beings. Might one not argue that this is characteristically and distinctively human activity? I'm not certain that *Beyond Therapy* directly addresses such a claim, but we can see what its answer would be. By thinking of our humanity only as willed freedom over limitations and not also as finite embodiedness, we lose—or at least diminish—something essential to our created nature.

I used to be a rather regular watcher of *Baseball Tonight* on ESPN. Near the end of the program there were always two segments showing brief clips from that day's games. One segment, "Going, Going, Gone," simply showed one home run after another—displays of power and strength. The other—and by my lights more interesting—segment was called "Web Gems." There we saw the best defensive plays of the day—not just one feat

40

of power after another, but graceful displays of human beings at work. After a while the home runs all look pretty much alike; each of the web gems has its own distinctive excellence. They are not just superior activity in general; they are the flourishing activity of particular persons. Something like that, if I may be allowed such a proletarian illustration, gets at a bit of what *Beyond Therapy* has in mind. Its contention is that enhancement should concern us primarily because it threatens to diminish the humanly excellent character of what we do. Although *Beyond Therapy* does not put it this way, one might say that we have not been created to be well-functioning machines or even animals governed largely by instinct. Human excellence calls for something more difficult to achieve—not the loving disposition or graceful accomplishment produced by a pill or an injection, but the care for others and the excellent performance that develops over time through the training and discipline of our passions, desires, and capabilities. Perhaps, then, one reason to worry about biotechnical enhancement is that it might fail to honor and uphold the peculiar character of our created humanity.

RECONCILED LIFE

Michael Sandel's approach, although it draws on many of the same examples and shares many of *Beyond Therapy*'s concerns, identifies the deepest problem with enhancement differently. Although diminished agency is a genuine reason for concern, Sandel argues that the chief problem is almost the opposite—what he terms "hyperagency." "The problem is not the drift to mechanism but the drive to mastery. And what the drive to mastery misses, and may even destroy, is an appreciation of the gifted character of human powers and achievements."

As I noted earlier, *Beyond Therapy* explores enhancement in four different areas of life—examining our desire to produce better children, ageless bodies, happy souls, and superior performance. I am attending especially though not exclusively to attempts to improve our performance, whereas Sandel's primary focus is, I would say, the desire to produce better children, and that may be the area of enhancement that raises most obviously his concern about hyperagency. But he does not ignore the topic of superior performance, and there too he is concerned about the drive to mastery at least as much as the drift to mechanism.

Sandel does grant the validity of *Beyond Therapy*'s standpoint. How do we know when we are simply cultivating our legitimate gifts (as all of us may) or when, on the other hand, we are corrupting them by the use of enhancement techniques? His answer, repeated several times, is that it depends on whether these techniques "perfect or obscure the skills essential to the game." We want to perform and compete in such a way that we are participating in a "sport," not a "spectacle." This goes some way toward sharing the concerns of *Beyond Therapy*. For we can only distinguish in this way between sport and spectacle if we have some sense of what it means for us to be fully involved agents participating in the action. Thus, Sandel's focus on the dangers of a drive to mastery need not mean that we lose *Beyond Therapy*'s worries about how enhancement might diminish the character of our created humanity. His concern complements rather than replaces *Beyond Therapy*'s approach.

At the same time, we should not for a moment lose the additional insight his perspective contributes. The drive to mastery that is present in many of our attempts at enhancement displays and encourages a disposition that is, he believes, morally problematic. It expresses a willfulness and "an impulse to rail against the given" that is "the deepest source of the moral trouble with enhancement." We seek, even if not always self-consciously, to master our world and be self-sufficient. Sandel's characteristic way of making this point is to say that we lose, or at least endanger, a sense of the "giftedness" of life. We begin to imagine that our talents and powers are the result of our own doing, and we encourage ourselves to think of the world as available for shaping in accord with our ever more expansive desires and dreams.

For many readers it is probably hard not to hear this as a claim grounded in religious belief. A failure to see the giftedness of life is surely part of what Christians and Jews have meant by sin. Sandel acknowledges that his language of giftedness might easily be taken to express a religious sensibility, which he does not reject. But he also suggests that there may be other, nonreligious grounds for declining to think of the world as indefinitely malleable to our desires. Gratitude for our accomplishments can perhaps get along without metaphysical underpinnings any more developed than a kind of natural piety for what is given. "We commonly speak of an athlete's gift or a musician's, without making any assumption about whether or not the gift comes from God. What we mean is simply that the talent in question is not wholly the athlete's or the musician's own doing; whether he has nature, fortune, or God to thank for it, the talent is an endowment that exceeds his control." Even if this is true, we can see why religious thinkers might appropriate Sandel's approach as a way of expressing some of their own beliefs.

The drive to mastery embedded in enhancement carries with it several moral costs, which Sandel nicely develops. Those who do not think of themselves as gifted may lack the kind of humility needed to restrain their aims and projects. Lacking the humility that can relinquish control, we prefer "a world inhospitable to the unbidden, a gated community writ large." Moreover, thinking of ourselves as self-made and self-sufficient, we can easily lose a sense of solidarity with those who are less fortunate and less gifted than we. "A lively sense of the contingency of our gifts" provides the link that connects humility with solidarity.

Perhaps more important still is the way in which the drive to mastery may expand our sense of human responsibility to a point that loses the true meaning of our humanity. We see here why Sandel tends to think that the deepest problem raised by enhancement is not diminished agency but hyperagency—"the explosion, not the erosion, of responsibility." Making so much of life an arena governed by choice and will creates a burden of responsibility perhaps greater than human beings are meant to bear. The control we hope to exercise may actually reflect the deeply disordered character of human life, a disorder that in Jewish and Christian terms is unsurprising. Our lives are, after all, deeply distorted by sin.

We should remember, of course, that, just as picturing Satan with horns and pitchfork may blind us to him when he actually appears, so also warnings about hyperagency might encourage us to think only in terms of large-scale political programs or social movements. In fact, however, being blind to the giftedness of life may also readily undermine many of our everyday activities—being a parent or a spouse, accepting the inevitable decline of old age in ourselves or those we love, recognizing the limits even of our accomplishments, keeping in mind (as Chesterton put it) that it is not familiarity but comparison that breeds contempt. Thus, the thirst that drives large-scale enhancement projects can also corrupt many of the most important aspects of ordinary life.

Near the very end of his discussion Sandel offers a (to me) fascinating suggestion about what it was that gave rise to our age of genetic enhancement. We have tended to think that it grew unplanned from the great strides made in modern medicine. First we learned to cure disease in new ways, and then we realized that similar techniques might be used in ways that go "beyond therapy" for the perfecting of human nature. "But," Sandel suggests, "that may have the story backward." It could be that present at the creation of the genetic age was disordered desire. The age of genetic enhancement may be "the ultimate expression of our resolve to see ourselves astride the world." In short, a vision of a promised future, a future that would be the result of our own achievement and mastery, may lie at the root of this biotechnical movement.

We have, then, two reasons—complementary and not competing—for drawing back somewhat from the lure of enhancement. One approach explores the character of distinctively human activity, inviting us to affirm our created nature—to see even in its limits and vulnerability what is distinctively human. A second approach explores the human tendency to overreach, a tendency that surely contributes to much of the brokenness of a world in need of reconciliation. Thus, *Beyond Therapy* might be said to encourage us to understand and uphold our created nature in its integrity. *The Case against Perfection* might be read as depicting a world so broken by our desire for self-sufficiency that only God's reconciling action can begin to restore it.

Interestingly, however, neither of these concerns points us toward the future. Yet, if Sandel's closing suggestion is correct, at the root of the enhancement project may be a thirst to control and shape human destiny. This reminds us that the form of God's action in the history of redemption is threefold. We need, then, to consider what the future God promises may add to our consideration of enhancement, and, to be sure, how it may complicate our reflections.

REDEEMED LIFE

When we turn now to think about that desired (and promised) future, neither *Beyond Therapy* nor *The Case against Perfection* will be a sufficient guide. We are pretty much on our own. The Israelite prophet envisions a day when those

> who wait for the LORD shall renew their strength,
> they shall mount up with wings like eagles,
> they shall run and not be weary,
> they shall walk and not faint.

If we are to hold together the three moments in the history of redemption, we need to try to think of that promised future not as post-humanity but as perfected humanity. God responds to our refusal to see ourselves as gifted not simply by restoring the integrity of a corrupted creation but, as Barth writes, "with the revelation of a perfection concealed even in the original creation in its integrity. He does not only make the sick whole, but gives him a share in the hope of everlasting life." This, surely, is to be better than well.

But it is also to introduce a complicating factor into our attempt to evaluate the enhancement project. For this means that the promised future brings not just restoration of human agency but also renewal—agency of a sort we have not previously experienced. Thinking in these terms, Oliver O'Donovan has written that when the promised future breaks into our world at Easter, we are, on the one hand, helped to honor "the beauty and order of the life that was the creator's gift to his creation and is restored there." But, on the other hand, we are also turned "from the empty tomb to a new moment of participation in God's work and being."

This new moment comes to us not simply as a development of the past but as the advent of God's promised future. Theologians have sometimes distinguished between two different ways of talking about the future. We may speak of it as *futurum*, a development that draws out potential already present. Or we may speak of it as *adventus*, which comes to us not out of the past but as something new. Jürgen Moltmann makes the point nicely with reference to Revelation 1:4. It reads, "Grace to you and peace from him who is and who was and who is to come." We might expect, Moltmann observes, a slightly different formula: "him who is and who was and who will be." But the verse speaks not of the one who will be as he has been in the past but of the one who is to come. "God's future is not that he will be as he was and is, but that he is on the move and coming towards the world."

We have to ask ourselves, then, what might this divine *adventus* mean for the way we think about enhancement? Will it permit us to rest content simply with delineating the nature of created human agency or underscoring the hubris that distorts human life and must be overcome by God's reconciling work? Once we acknowledge that what God promises is a new creation, we may be unsure how to proceed. We can perhaps—even if just barely—imagine what human agency restored to its created character would be like. But can we pour any content into the promise of an entirely renewed humanity?

At the very least this suggests that even if we see enormous dangers in the push for enhancement, even if, together with Sandel, we detect in it "the ultimate expression of our resolve to see ourselves astride the world," we cannot respond simply by falling back into our finitude. Robert Song is right to argue that we should not "warmly embrace human limitations without a murmur of protest." In part we should not because the desire to transcend some givens of our finite condition is itself a legitimate aspect of our created nature. Just as important, however, is the fact that God does not simply repeat himself. Something new breaks into our world at Easter. It directs us back to a world restored. It also directs us forward, toward a world renewed. "*This* perishable nature must put on the imperishable," as St. Paul writes in 1 Corinthians. How shall we think about that renewed humanity, and what, if anything, can it teach us about enhancement?

I have already said that we are pretty much on our own when we try to think about the future God has promised. Pretty much, but not entirely. "We can," as Eric Mascall once put it, "dimly see what it will involve if we look at the human being in whom it has already happened"—that is, the resurrected Jesus. Doing so offers a hint of how we might think about the perfected humanity at least of those who share in his life. The transcendence of which Jesus's resurrection is the first fruit is promised not as escape from bodily life but as the hope of a body transformed. In some way or other it must involve not just our disembodied spirit but the whole of our being. Can we say anything about that transformed, enhanced existence—and, even more important, does what we say have any implications for our attitude toward enhancement here and now?

To say too much here would be to lose the tentativeness that seems appropriate; yet, to understand appropriate tentativeness to mean, essentially, silence, would be to cut these reflections a bit short. But, although enhancement there will surely be, I am going to interpret this last chapter in the history of redemption chiefly as an invitation to caution about enhancement projects here and now—and that for roughly three sorts of reasons. I state them here briefly and will then try to develop them at least a little. First, there are aspects of bodily life that cut so deeply into our personal identity that perhaps we should not seek to alter them, much less enhance them. Second, the perfected humanity of God's promised future cannot be our own achievement and, hence, should perhaps not be the product of our manipulation. And third, the end state toward which we move in the history of redemption is one of contentment; perhaps we should begin to practice it here and now.

When Christians have thought about the future God promises, they have often focused on what it will mean spiritually. Perhaps unsurprisingly, they have supposed that in that promised future, sharing in the beatific vision, our knowing will be elevated. Not necessarily in the sense that we would then know whatever there is to be known, but in the sense that we would attain a "connatural" knowledge of God—the kind of knowing that comes from sharing God's life rather than simply looking at it from the outside. We should not, though, picture this in too monochromatic a fashion. In C. S. Lewis's *Great Divorce* George MacDonald puts in an appearance, instructing the narrator in the nature of the redeemed life. Each of the saints, MacDonald says, will see some things better than others, and, when they do, they will want to share what they see. In that way the vision of all will be enhanced.

Christians have also supposed that in the resurrected life peace and joy will be undisturbed—without, evidently, the aid of Prozac. "In that soul where divine love reigns, and is in lively exercise," Jonathan Edwards says in the fifteenth of his *Charity* sermons, "nothing can raise a storm." Closely related to these enhancements would be the kind of moral perfection Edwards imagines must be present in the "world of love" that is heaven. Morally, those who share in the resurrected life of Christ are, clearly, better than well. "With respect to the degree of their love, it is perfect. . . . Their love shall be without any remains of a contrary principle." Thinking perhaps of the passage from Isaiah that I cited earlier, Edwards writes, "The soul which is winged with love shall have no weight tied to the feet to hinder its flight."

However delightful and desirable such enhancements of mind and character would be, they retain a kind of "spiritual" quality that says relatively little about the promised future of created *bodies*. Taken alone, such promised enhancements might even seduce us into supposing that the body is not involved in the perfection God promises. But to think that would be to lose what was my starting point—namely, the stories of the resurrected Jesus. Were it not for the testimony of those who saw him we would have little reason to suppose that the redemption God promises extends to our bodies.

But clearly, those witnesses did not think of the resurrection as purely spiritual. What they describe is an entirely new mode of being, which is both continuous and discontinuous with bodily life as we know it. Jesus's resurrected body can continue to be present in the natural world we inhabit, related to us in both space and time; yet, it rides nature and is not ridden by it. This is not simply a restoration of creation but, rather, a genuinely new work of God that nevertheless reveals what Barth calls "a perfection concealed even in the original creation in its integrity." It is a little more like the gutting and rebuilding of a house than the building of an entirely new one. Quite obviously, our attempts to describe this are likely to be halting and inadequate. As C. S. Lewis once put it in an oft-quoted passage, "I think our present outlook might be like that of a small boy who, on being told that the sexual act was the highest bodily pleasure, should immediately ask whether you ate chocolates at the same time. . . . The boy knows chocolate: he does not know the positive thing that excludes it." When it comes to imagining the perfect bodies of God's new creation, we are all like the small boy.

No doubt we are naturally inclined to imagine that any bodily defects present in this life will no longer be present in the risen and redeemed bodies of the new creation. In heaven, Edwards says, "there shall be none appearing with any defects either natural or moral." With some hesitation, however, I am inclined to agree only in part. With respect to our moral (and spiritual) perfection, it is difficult to imagine those who are in any way still hostile to God, those who are unwilling to bend the knee in adoration of God, or those whose loves remain disordered being able to love God with all their heart, soul, strength, and mind. So, then, no moral defects in our perfected humanity.

But, while granting that these questions admit of no certain answer, I tend to think we should not necessarily say the same with respect to all defects of nature. After all, the marks of nails and spear remain in the body of the resurrected Christ, but these bodily "defects"—if that is the right word—have been taken into a life of glory. They mark the continuity that exists between the Jesus who lived and died, and the Jesus who now lives as the Lamb that was slain. They are central to his identity, which is why Thomas was invited to see and touch them.

I am wading into deep and troubling waters here, but I suspect that some bodily defects may touch us so deeply as to shape who we are. If the stump that should have been my leg has shaped the person I am throughout my life, are we certain that even in the new creation this person should now have two legs? If my child has from birth had Down syndrome, if it is *that* child whom I have loved, and if she has in return loved me in her characteristic way, are we certain that even in the new creation she should be free · of the limitations that come along with Down's? I am, of course, in danger of becoming like the small boy who knows only the pleasure of chocolates, but perhaps we have to run that risk.

I said near the outset of this essay that I would try to avoid the thorny problem of distinguishing therapy from enhancement, and I have now brought upon myself the complications it involves. After all, I would not say that here and now we should simply forego therapeutic attempts to cure or ameliorate defects of the body. If we could cure Down's prenatally, no doubt we should. But there are many imponderables here. If my daughter lives for thirty years with Down syndrome, if that is who she is in relation to me and all others, is there some point at which, even in this life, we should not try to "cure" her condition? How long must she live as an individual with Down's before attempting to "cure" her would be more like obliterating her? If such questions make sense, then I am not certain why her redeemed body should be not only cured but also enhanced. There is, at least, reason here for caution, reason grounded in aspects of our bodily life that cut very deeply into our identity.

There is also a second reason for caution. Recall how *Beyond Therapy*, attempting to characterize humanly excellent action, described it in terms of a unity of doer with deed, a unity and wholeness not naturally given to us, since we are divided within ourselves. For *Beyond Therapy* humanly excellent action is, therefore, a notable achievement of which the other animals are not capable. We might wonder, though, whether the discord we often experience in action can really be overcome entirely by anything properly characterized as our achievement. Robert Song seems right to say of the resurrected (perfected and enhanced) body that "whatever . . . [it] is, it cannot be the end product of human manipulation." Whatever enhanced capacities the new creation might offer, they cannot be entirely our own achievement. And since they are not, we can hardly be too confident about our efforts to imagine or produce them.

It follows that where our understanding is so limited so also should be our efforts to manipulate. Wisely, therefore, C. S. Lewis observed in *Miracles*, "Mystics have got as far in contemplation of God as the point at which the senses are banished: the further point, at which they will be put back again, has (to the best of my knowledge) been reached by no one." This is as it should be. The perfection of our bodies belongs to a *history* of redemption, a history not yet concluded, a history that we do not control. And if it is such a history, perhaps "perfection" is not quite the right way—a bit too static, a bit lacking in diversity—to describe the goal at which this history aims. Perhaps the language of glory, which is biblical language, should be preferred. The history of redemption is, St. Paul writes in 2 Corinthians, already at work in our world as we, "beholding the glory of the Lord, are being changed into his likeness from one degree of glory to another." Which brings me to yet a third reason for caution.

Edwards was confident that there would still be degrees of glory in heaven. What there will not be, however, is envy on the part of those who are lesser in glory. In this he was simply reworking an idea from Augustine's *City of God*: "But what will be the grades of honour and glory here [i.e., in heaven], appropriate to degrees of merit? Who is capable of imagining them, not to speak of describing them? But there will be such distinctions; of that there can be no doubt. And here also that blessed City will find in itself a great blessing, in that no inferior will feel envy of his superior. . . . And so, although one will have a gift inferior to another, he will also have the compensatory gift of contentment with what he has." And if content, evidently not thirsting to be enhanced. Here, at least, that thirst for mastery and its accompanying ingratitude for the gifts given us, a thirst that Sandel thought he discerned as a motivating force in our culture's desire for enhancement, will have been uprooted and overcome. Perhaps we should say that when we have received the promised gift of perfected humanity, we will no longer desire it as our own achievement.

This gives us a clue about how to think of enhancement here and now. We need not reject out of hand every attempt at enhancement, though we should retain a healthy skepticism about our ability to distinguish genuine enhancement from the simulacra our disordered desires are likely to imagine. Perhaps there can be moments when aiming at enhancement is an appropriate exercise of our created freedom or even an anticipation of a renewed world. But it should hardly be our central concern. For we are on our way to a state of contentment. Along the way in this history of redemption, we should seek to free ourselves from the thirst that undermines the genuine human agency described in *Beyond Therapy*, a thirst that also blinds us, as Sandel emphasizes, to the giftedness that marks our lives. Surely though, if not here and now, then one day there will be a place for enhancement in this history, because in some way or other it must be part of the future God has promised. In what way or other? Well, perhaps it does no harm if we now and again allow our imaginations to roam a bit, considering possible future enhancements—as did Augustine, Edwards, and Lewis, and as I myself have done—but in order then, in Lewis's words, "to make room for a more complete and circumspect agnosticism."

BIBLIOGRAPHY

Barth, Karl. *Church Dogmatics*, II/1. Edinburgh: T. & T. Clark, 1957. (See pages 506–12.)

————. *Church Dogmatics*, III/4. Edinburgh: T. & T. Clark, 1961. (See pages 24–26.)

Edwards, Jonathan. *Ethical Writings*. Edited by Paul Ramsey. Works of Jonathan Edwards 8. New Haven: Yale University Press, 1989.

Lewis, C. S. *Miracles: A Preliminary Study*. New York: Macmillan, 1947.

Mascall, E. L. *Grace and Glory*. New York: Morehouse-Barlow, 1961.

Moltmann, Jürgen. *The Coming of God: Christian Eschatology*. Minneapolis: Fortress, 1966.

O'Donovan, Oliver. *Self, World, and Time: An Induction*. Grand Rapids: Eerdmans, 2013.

President's Council on Bioethics. *Beyond Therapy: Biotechnology and the Pursuit of Happiness*. New York: HarperPerennial, 2003.

Sandel, Michael J. *The Case against Perfection: Ethics in the Age of Genetic Engineering*. Cambridge: Belknap Press of Harvard University Press, 2007.

Song, Robert. *Human Genetics: Fabricating the Future*. Cleveland: Pilgrim, 2002.

4

Stem Cells and Torture[1]

L et's start with stem cells. That may seem a strange place to begin thinking about torture, but many bioethical issues are at least as controversial and disputed as is torture. Among the most controversial in recent years has been research that destroys embryos in order to procure stem cells for use in regenerative medicine. Those who oppose embryonic stem cell research have, in my view, made the right moral choice. The logic of that choice is worth examining, however, before we turn more directly to the issue of torture, for it is a choice that comes with certain costs.

It is still much too soon to say for sure whether the promise for regenerative medicine that some see in embryo-destructive research will be fulfilled or will turn out to be a dead end. Perhaps other approaches—using induced pluripotent stem cells or altered nuclear transfer—will make better scientific progress without the destruction of embryos, demonstrating that at least sometimes we can have our cake and eat it too. But perhaps not. Maybe these other approaches will fail to cure or ameliorate suffering from serious degenerative diseases and embryo-destructive research will, in fact, turn out to be the "gold standard" its defenders often call it.

Even if things were to turn out that way, it would not mean that opponents of embryonic stem cell research had been wrong. It would simply mean that they had accepted the cost to which their moral beliefs committed

1. An earlier version of this essay appeared in *The Weekly Standard*, June 8, 2009.

them. They do not think that good results are the only—or even the most important—factor in determining how we ought to live. However fervently and sincerely they may hope that we find ways to relieve the condition of those who suffer, they do not take the further moral step of concluding that any and every avenue to that good end may be used. If this means that some suffering that could be relieved is not, then that is the cost, however regrettable, that a commitment to act rightly will sometimes exact.

DOING AND ACCOMPLISHING

This distinction, between what we *do* and what we *accomplish*, marks one of the fault lines in moral reasoning, and it reemerges time and again in bioethical argument. This was seen clearly and stated directly and forcefully when bioethics first burst upon the scene in this country. Thus, in *The Patient as Person*, one of the classic early works in bioethics, Paul Ramsey underscored the fundamental moral point: "There may be valuable scientific knowledge which it is morally impossible to obtain. There may be truths which would be of great and lasting benefit to mankind if they could be discovered, but which cannot be discovered without systematic and sustained violations of legitimate moral imperatives."

Embryonic stem cell research itself could not at that time have been on Ramsey's radar, prescient though he was in many ways. However, the ethics of medical research more generally surely was. A subject that received sustained attention in those early years of bioethics, it was the topic of a long and complicated chapter in *The Patient as Person*. The thread that holds together the chapter's complications is the moral stance I have noted. The fact that both researchers and subjects are human persons "places an independent moral limit [independent, that is, of all possible good results flowing out of the research] upon the fashion in which the rest of mankind can be made the ultimate beneficiary of these procedures." That independent limit is the requirement that research subjects be able to give and actually do give a free and informed consent to their participation. If they cannot, the research ought not to be done, however beneficial for others it might be—or so Ramsey, at any rate, believed.

Similar themes were sounded at that time by the Jewish philosopher Hans Jonas, once described by Ramsey as "a person to me of exemplary moral wisdom." In "Philosophical Reflections on Experimenting with Human Subjects," a profound article that continues to repay careful study,

53

Jonas considered the claim that a society "could not afford" to forego research that might improve and save lives—and could not, therefore, be too insistent on moral limits that would impede such research. His reflections on that sort of claim, a claim that might come all too readily to the lips of any of us, are bracing. "Of course" a society can afford to lose members through death. If diseases "continue to exact their toll at the normal rate of incidence . . . society can go on flourishing in every way."

To make medical progress through human experimentation is surely desirable; yet, Jonas wrote, such improvement is "an optional goal" and "has nothing sacred about it." What, then, *is* sacred? Each individual person, any one of whom we might be tempted to misuse in the cause of progress for others.

We should not, however, make Jonas's position simpler than it was. Improving society through research is always desirable but also always optional. Hence, such research is subject to what Ramsey called independent moral limits. They may retard our progress, but society can afford this and, indeed, morally must afford it. But what if the issue is not improving but, more starkly, preserving society? Jonas was prepared to acknowledge that there are "examples of what, in sober truth, society cannot afford." It cannot afford to let an epidemic "rage unchecked." Some epidemics are acute— as, for example, the Black Death was. Others are public calamities of a more chronic kind—as, for example, "the life-sapping ravages of endemic malaria" may be. Of these possibilities Jonas wrote, "A society as a whole can truly not 'afford' such situations, and they may call for extraordinary remedies, including, perhaps, the invasion of private sacrosanctities." Jonas did not think of this as a matter of numbers alone, since, as he noted, there is also a sense in which society cannot afford a single injustice or violation of rights. Still, there might be cases "critically affecting the whole condition, present and future, of the community" that could constitute something like a state of emergency in which disaster could be averted only through "extraordinary means" of experimentation—means otherwise forbidden.

STEM CELLS

Think now of our more recent disputes over embryonic stem cell research. However great the promise of such research for relief of suffering and prevention of death, the fact that we continue to suffer and die is not an emergency. If we take to describing that sad fact of life as a crisis or emergency, there will be no end to what we might contemplate doing in the cause of medical progress. Our desire to *accomplish* good results will have swamped any moral limits on what we *do* in pursuit of that goal. And, more generally, this should make us wary of the martial language—a "war on cancer"—still all too common in our thinking about medicine.

The policy for federal funding of embryonic stem cell research adopted by then President Bush attempted both to recognize necessary moral limits and acknowledge complexities. That policy—which permitted funding of research only on stem cell lines derived from embryos destroyed prior to the President's decision—aimed at acknowledging the good of research, but in a way that would not encourage further destruction of embryos. From the standpoint of opponents of the research, it ran the moral risk of complicity in an evil deed. From the standpoint of proponents of the research, it incurred considerable moral cost, because of the limits it put in place. At least in my mind, there was considerable wisdom in the policy. We should acknowledge independent moral limits on how we pursue the goals we desire, and, therefore, we need not hesitate to argue that research in regenerative medicine ought to proceed by means that do not destroy the tiny human beings we all once were: embryos. But there will be costs—moral costs—to such a choice, for medical progress in regenerative medicine may be slower than it could be. What we accomplish, or decline to try to accomplish, does matter morally.

TORTURE

The logic of that choice, as well as its complexities, should not be forgotten as we turn now to reflect upon torture. Even here, though, I begin rather far away from disputes that arose after the terrorist attacks of 2001 and the ensuing warfare. There is a brief but fascinating discussion of torture in Helmut Thielicke's *Theological Ethics*. To appreciate its significance we must keep in mind the difficulty—shared by Thielicke—that a certain kind of contemporary Lutheran theology has had with offering any moral guidance and direction.

Why should it be so hard? Because even the very "best" of us never reach a point at which we can with confidence seek God's judgment upon our behavior. If the best and the worst of us are equally sinners before God, it may seem beside the point to distinguish better from worse actions. (To give him his due, we should note that Thielicke was better than his theory during the years of the Nazi regime.)

If the point of theological ethics is not to distinguish better from worse actions, what is its point? It is to direct us away from our own (always tainted) attempts to distinguish right from wrong and to direct us toward reliance on God's mercy. Or, in Thielicke's rather more passionate language, the point of theological ethics is to uncover our Babylonian hearts and shatter our illusion that we might lay claim to being righteous. In the dark of night, all cats are gray, and what really counts is our justification before God, a justification that depends not a bit on anything we do, but entirely on God's grace.

Whatever power there may be in such a theological vision—and there is some, as any reader of Thielicke knows—it will have difficulty saying of any deed that its very doing is incompatible with righteousness before God. How very striking, therefore, that in certain "confrontations with transcendence" Thielicke himself found examples of "limits which cannot be transgressed," instances in which there is only one course of action compatible with righteousness before God. This may be an inconsistency in his thinking; if so, it is a felicitous and instructive inconsistency.

The first example he gives of such a limit is the invitation to accomplish some great good through blasphemy. My concern, though, is with his second example of "direct confrontation with transcendence." This happens when the personhood of another human being, "the bearer of an alien dignity" and "the direct representation of transcendence," is at stake. "Of man's personhood too we may say, figuratively [as the prophet reports the LORD says of Israel], 'He who touches it touches the apple of God's eye.'"

How might we thus touch the apple of God's eye? And what might tempt us to do so? Thielicke has in mind circumstances "in which everything (the fate and success of our movement, perhaps the lives of our companions, wives, children, and even our very nation) depends upon the obtaining of certain information. In such cases the question inevitably arises whether we may obtain this information by means either of torture or of procedures of interrogation involving the use of certain truth drugs." (For the moment, I leave torture undefined. That Thielicke can group these two means of acquiring information together helps us see what he thinks is at stake, what he means by a "confrontation with transcendence.")

In torture we seek to overcome another person's conscientious resistance to our will. We aim to "break the conscience which is commanding him to keep silence." This differs from what Thielicke calls "temptation by desire," which seeks to work "by way of the man's own decisions." Nor can torture be equated with coercion, with an attempt to force a decision out of the person. Torture seeks to inflict pain severe enough to eliminate the ego, to bypass "the sphere of decision altogether." It seeks, we might say, to turn the person—a subject—into an object, a thing.

Seeing this, we can understand why Thielicke groups torture with the use of a truth serum, which does not inflict pain but which also attempts to bypass the sphere of decision. His fundamental category is not torture but dehumanization. Temptation and coercion attack—but without bypassing or subverting—the person, and they may sometimes be permitted or even required. Torture and truth serum bypass—we might say, "thingify"—the person, taking away "the personal right to decision." But if the human person is a representation of transcendence, it is the transcendent that has then become our target. A Christian "owes to the world," Thielicke writes, "the public confession that he is one who is committed, 'bound,' and hence not 'capable of [just] anything.' If we make ourselves fundamentally unpredictable, i.e., if as Christians we think that torture is at least conceivable—perhaps under the exigencies of an extreme situation—we thereby reduce man to the worth of a convertible means, divest him of the *imago Dei*, and so deny the first commandment. This denial can never be a possible alternative."

In his *Apologia Pro Vita Sua*, John Henry Cardinal Newman wrote, "The Catholic Church holds it better for the sun and moon to drop from heaven, for the earth to fail, and for all the many millions on it to die of starvation in extremest agony, as far as temporal affliction goes, than that one soul, I will not say, should be lost, but should commit one single venial sin, should tell one willful untruth, or should steal one poor farthing without excuse." I am not certain I want to agree with either Newman or Thielicke; or, at least, I want to think later about distinctions analogous to those raised by Hans Jonas with respect to medical experimentation. However, it is, to say the very least, instructive to find Thielicke, whose brand of Lutheranism always flirts with antinomianism, insisting, at least in this instance, what we *do* counts for more than what we *accomplish*, and insisting upon it in a way as relentlessly demanding as Newman's.

It is important that we acknowledge just how demanding it is—important, that is, to acknowledge the cost of giving moral priority to doing rather than accomplishing. "Saints should always be judged guilty until they are proved innocent," Orwell wrote of Gandhi, and Orwell's own inclination was to think of the saint's demanding standards as, finally, "anti-human." We may disagree with him, but we should be willing to count the cost of doing so.

Thus, while it may be disturbing to hear former Vice President Cheney calling for full disclosure of the beneficial results of enhanced interrogation methods used in secret during his tenure in office, he was quite right to do so. If we wish to renounce those tactics, we should estimate as best we can the cost of doing so. Even those who reject all utilitarian calculations should not deny the truth in utilitarianism: namely, that consequences do matter.

Or again, it is far too easy an exercise in cost-counting to say with confidence that torture never works. And there are, in fact, persuasive counterexamples. It worked for the French in Algeria (though it is useful to remember that, in the longer run, they lost that struggle), and it has worked on occasion for Israeli authorities. Probably it would always be hard to predict whether torture would work in a given instance, but that is different from the far less persuasive claim that it never extracts useful or reliable information.

It is those holding political office who must pay special attention to consequences. Indeed, that's why they hold office: to focus on what will, within the limits of their power, secure the well-being of the fellow citizens whom they serve. They may—and sometimes should—authorize us to do what none of us ought to do in our purely private capacities. They may authorize us, that is, to aim to kill those who do injustice or who threaten our life or way of life.

Government may punish—and even, in certain circumstances, kill—not because it is itself "lord" of life and death but because it is the authorized agent of the God who is that Lord. But there are always limits on how government should carry out its retributive and punitive purposes. Even in the extreme case of war we see such limits in the firmly entrenched rule (which is moral, and not just legal) that we may not take aim at noncombatants. We might have good reason to target civilians, thinking thereby to break the enemy's will to resist, and the United States has sometimes done this—notably in the bombing of German cities and in the use of the atomic bomb against Japan (not to mention General Sherman's march to the sea). But those actions, however laudable the cause they served and whatever good results they may have accomplished, undermine our sense that war as a human activity should be a test of strength, not of will.

Hence, what a terrorist does is quite different from what a soldier does. The essential feature of the terrorist's action is that it deliberately (and, generally, at random) targets civilians. Terrorists do so simply to instill fear, and, as Michael Walzer has written, "in its modern manifestations, terror is the totalitarian form of war and politics." It recognizes no limits on the violence that can be enacted in a good cause, and it subsumes individuals entirely into their political communities—treating us as if we belonged to those communities to the whole extent of our being.

Our obligations to captured terrorists are not, therefore, quite the same as our obligations to captured soldiers, to whom "benevolent quarantine" is owed. (This is a point about our moral, not our legal, obligations. If the Geneva Conventions do not recognize such a distinction, they miss something of moral importance.) The quarantine of terrorists need not be so benevolent. Indeed, once we begin to think about the difference between a captured soldier and a captured terrorist, we might well be puzzled about what we owe the terrorist.

After all, a captured terrorist may not only have carried out an attack in the past; we may have good reason to believe he is planning an attack still to be carried out in the future. If we caught him in the act of doing it, we could kill him in order to protect his innocent victims. Now that we have caught him before that next act—but have not caught all others engaged with him in planning it—can we do nothing to him to protect the innocents at whom the plans he knows and shares in are taking aim? Government authorities may surely prey upon his desires and weaknesses in seeking information from him. Likewise, he may be coerced in a variety of ways, using such coercion to "motivate" him to cooperate. But subjecting him to experiences that simply break his will, that turn him into a thing no longer able to decide (in response to either temptation or coercion) is a different matter entirely.

No rule can tell us precisely when we have crossed the line that separates justified temptation or coercion from actions (whatever we call them) that are not justified. Clearly, the issue is not only infliction of pain. Enforced nudity, though not in itself necessarily painful, nonetheless "thingifies" a person. Being slapped, even hard, does not (or so it seems to me). Being forced to sit in one's urine or feces "thingfies" a person. Being forced to listen for long periods of time to loud (and perhaps offensive) music does not, or so it seems to me. None of these should be done to a captured soldier, but perhaps some of them could legitimately be done to a captured terrorist. Part of our problem is that we—as a people—have had as much difficulty sustaining an honest conversation free of posturing about this question as we have in the case of stem cell research.

STEM CELLS AND TORTURE: WRONGS AND HARMS

To return now to the matter of stem cells, suppose what was needed was not an entire industry devoted to the use and destruction of embryos in an ongoing program of research but, instead, just three specific embryos. Produce and destroy them, and we position ourselves for continual progress in the war against degenerative diseases. Draw back, and we forgo all such good results. It's a hypothetical with no purchase on reality, of course, but I have often wondered what my answer to it would be.

In theory, the answer ought to be clear. If human beings were simply members of our species, it might sometimes make sense to sacrifice one or another of them for the sake of the species as a whole. But human beings are not just members of the species or parts of a whole. Each human being is a "someone" who belongs to no earthly community to the whole extent of his being. That is why we are not interchangeable. Even if the "value" of a thousand people is greater than the value of one, the thousand are not more than one in personal dignity.

Thus, the answer should be clear. As Hans Jonas observed, society can afford to regard medical progress as optional if the price of such progress is infringing upon the dignity of human life. But Jonas also believed there were some things that "in sober truth, society cannot afford." Writing about medical research, his example was an epidemic raging unchecked. It is not silly to think of terrorist activity—which intends, after all, to undermine all settled social life by returning us to something rather like Hobbes's state of nature—as a political parallel.

Epidemics may, Jonas observed, be acute (the Black Death) or chronic (endemic malaria). He was writing about medical experimentation, and he seems to mean that in the face of an acute epidemic, a society—in order to survive—might have to conscript research subjects. To do so violates our sense that people should be used as research subjects only with their consent. It transgresses that moral boundary in a time of emergency because, so it seems, society cannot afford not to. It is a boundary I can imagine myself crossing in dire circumstances. The captured terrorist still conspiring (if only through silence) in plans for further, imminent attacks is the political equivalent of an acute epidemic. And those who hold political office may be moved to step out into a moral no-man's-land in deciding what society can or cannot afford in the face of that threat.

Would I authorize that the captured terrorist be slapped around? Yes. Deprived of sleep for a time and disoriented? Yes. Waterboarded once? Now I begin to suspect that it is corrupting to try to answer that question in advance, as if there were a policy we could formulate to protect ourselves in a moral no-man's-land. But the answer must, I think, turn on whether doing it once would be more like an attempt at coercion, which is still a test of strength, or whether from the start it would aim to thingify the captured terrorist, trying to bypass altogether his capacity to decide. That brings us, however, to Thielicke's other, very different example: not the infliction of pain, but the use of truth serum. Would I authorize it in this circumstance? Perhaps again it is corrupting to try to answer that question in advance, but, to the degree one can, I suspect the answer is yes. But, then, why not just three embryos—were that, by hypothesis, all that were needed? In each case wrong, but very little harm, is done.

These questions and reflections have all grown out of Jonas's sense of what a society can or cannot afford in the face of an acute epidemic, which threatens its very ability to survive. Should we, perhaps, question that line of thinking? Why should it not be true of societies as much as individuals that how they live counts for more than how long? Is there anything sacred about the survival of our community—or any community? Surely not.

Saying that does not, however, solve the problem faced by those in political authority. For even if the continued survival of our society is not the highest moral good, they have been placed in authority precisely to see to the security and well-being of the society they serve. What choice have political leaders in the face of such an acute threat? If they will not or cannot step into the moral no-man's-land, they must probably resign—unless large numbers of us insist that they remain in office. But, of course, those who replace them may have fewer scruples and—as in Jesus's story about the house swept free of a demon into which seven yet more evil demons then enter—"the last state of that man becomes worse than the first."

What if we face not an acute but a chronic epidemic? My own sense is that this is quite a different matter, and Jonas was too quick to lump them together. It is one thing to step into a moral no-man's-land in the face of an acute emergency. But if the crisis continues indefinitely, it ceases to be an emergency and becomes everyday life. Not three embryos destroyed just once but an ongoing industry of embryo-destructive research, with which we make our peace on the ground that we do this in the face of the ongoing crisis of human suffering. We should reject the notion of a "war" against disease; it will turn out to justify transgressing most moral boundaries that present themselves. We need to learn again that it is not within our power to make ourselves, our society, or those we love secure. How easily we forget that our society and its way of life are fragile and delicate flowers. They are always at risk.

On October 22, 1939, at the Church of St. Mary the Virgin in Oxford, C. S. Lewis preached at evensong. To anxious undergraduates, many of whom would soon face death, and all of whom must have wondered what they were doing studying mathematics or metaphysics at a time when their nation was in mortal peril, Lewis said, "If we had foolish unchristian hopes about human culture, they are now shattered. If we thought we were building up a heaven on earth, if we looked for something that would turn the present world from a place of pilgrimage into a permanent city satisfying the soul of man, we are disillusioned, and not a moment too soon." Life, and our shared way of life, are always fragile and insecure. That is not a crisis; it is human history. And during our share of that history it will always be true that how, rather than how long, we live should be our central concern.

BIBLIOGRAPHY

Jonas, Hans. "Philosophical Reflections on Experimenting with Human Subjects." In *Philosophical Essays: From Ancient Creed to Technological Man*, 105–31. Englewood Cliffs, NJ: Prentice-Hall, 1974.

Orwell, George. "Reflections on Gandhi." In *A Collection of Essays*, 171–80. New York: Harcourt Brace Jovanovich, 1946.

Ramsey, Paul. *The Patient as Person: Explorations in Medical Ethics*. New Haven: Yale University Press, 1970.

Thielicke, Helmut. *Theological Ethics*. Vol. 1, *Foundations*. Philadelphia: Fortress, 1966.

Walzer, Michael. *Just and Unjust Wars*. New York: Basic Books, 1977.

II

Thinking Theologically:
Life's Beginning

5

The Future of Babymaking[1]

It was forty-five years ago, in his *Ethics of Genetic Control*, that Joseph Fletcher articulated clearly what the future of babymaking was going to be. Reproductive technologies can now do far more than was possible when Fletcher wrote, but not more than he could imagine. "Love making and baby making have been divorced," he wrote. "Sex is free from the contingencies and complications of reproduction, and sexual practice can now proceed on its own merits as an independent value in life."

Fletcher emphasized the importance of both choice and control in human reproduction, though it was never quite clear which of them was the more basic in his thinking. Asserting that human reproduction was now centered in will and choice rather than in our genitalia, he nevertheless was quite ready to require the "genetically unfortunate" to be sterilized and able without hesitation to assert that those who knowingly give birth to a "defective" child are "as guilty of wrongdoing as those who culpably contribute to a wrongful death."

We are now fast approaching a point at which a half-century's technological development may make Fletcher's imaginings sober reality. In an article in *The New York Review of Books* (September 25, 2014), Carl Djerassi suggests that in less than another half-century we can expect to see an increasing "divorce of coitus from reproduction." Due to the ever-increasing

---

1. An earlier version of this essay appeared in *Commonweal* 142.2 (January 23, 2015).

ability to freeze not only embryos but also a woman's eggs, in vitro fertilization (IVF) will no longer, he predicts, be used only by women with impaired fertility. Instead, it will become a desirable reproductive method even for women who experience no fertility problems. As if on cue, the *New York Times* reported that some companies—in particular, tech companies such as Facebook and Apple—have recently begun to offer a new "health benefit," covering a considerable portion of the expense of freezing eggs for women who work for the company. Djerassi also notes that women may even wish to be sterilized once their eggs have been retrieved—the better to enjoy sex without fear of an inconvenient pregnancy. There are at least two reasons, he thinks, why this scenario is by no means far-fetched.

In part, the opportunity to retrieve and freeze a relatively large number of eggs at an early age may offer a kind of insurance against future health or reproductive problems. Doing so would not commit a woman to using IVF in the future; she might still decide to conceive children in the old-fashioned way. But it would provide options for the future, enabling women to use their cache of stored eggs for reproductive purposes at a later age, whenever they feel the time is right. To be sure, embryo retrieval requiring hormonally induced superovulation carries some medical risks and possible complications during pregnancy that should not be underestimated. Djerassi's expectation that IVF will be used with increasing frequency by women with no fertility problems rests on the not unreasonable assumption that the procedures will continue to be improved and the risks lessened. It is hard to bet against medical advance, and, in addition, Djerassi also notes a point that has become rather standard in defense of new reproductive technologies—namely, that "normal coital reproduction at an advanced age carries its own risks." Evidently these are simply two ways, each with its pros and cons, of producing a desired result.

A second reason for Djerassi's prediction of increased IVF use even by women who have experienced no fertility problems is essentially eugenic. Screening for birth defects prior to implanting an embryo can become routine. "For many fertile women who plan on having no more than one or two children, and are prepared to pay for such information, this would be a major incentive to pursue the IVF route to conception rather than ordinary coitus." Fletcher would have understood. "Producing our children by 'sexual roulette' . . . simply taking 'pot luck' from random sexual combinations, is irresponsible," he wrote. Choice replaces chance and control replaces mystery—at least for those with the financial resources to seize the opportunity offered by reproductive technology.

There will be some, as there have always been, who will pooh-pooh any prediction that our future might be one in which coitus and reproduction are separated in the minds and lives of many people. At least in my experience a common response to predictions like Djerassi's has been a slightly worldly laugh and the observation that most people are surely likely to prefer the route of sexual intercourse. But that response assumes, of course, that babymaking via IVF (using frozen eggs or embryos) is still somehow connected to the experience of coitus. That response has not yet made the mental separation Djerassi foresees, imagining a very different world from the one to which we are accustomed. In the future world he anticipates these are simply two different things: sex for the fun of it, children if and when we choose and of the sort we choose.

A better and more thoughtful response would ask two questions about such a future world: Would it be good for children? Would it be good for sex?

Think first about children. Why should it matter how we produce them if, once we have them, we love them? In fact, might we not love all the more those whom we have taken pains to produce, those who are not simply the result of a passionate act that was probably not focused on the well-being of a possible future child? Perhaps so. At the very least, we need not deny that parents who use technology to produce their children—and, perhaps, even produce them to meet certain specifications—will love them. But that does not mean there is no cause for concern here.

One of the oldest distinctions in moral thought is between *doing* and *making*. Making occupies a great deal of our lives, as it should. We are in the world as people who have projects, people who seek to accomplish a variety of important aims and produce needed products. Yet, of course, we are not just makers or engineers; we are also doers who engage in a variety of activities whose worth is entirely independent of any product that results. Thus, we play, we worship, we admire the beautiful in sight or sound—and we make love. In such doings we are not seeking to accomplish something or produce some result. On the contrary, we exercise a certain generosity of spirit that takes us out of ourselves and testifies to goods whose worth cannot be measured in terms of goals accomplished or strategic plans carried out.

There may be countless ways to *make* a child; not all of them amount to *doing* the same thing. When a man and a woman give themselves to each other in the act of love, they are not undertaking a project intended to produce a child as the aimed-for result. They are not making anything, but they are doing something of great human significance. Perhaps they deeply desire a child, perhaps they hope that their lovemaking will have a child as its fruition. Still, that hoped-for child is not the object of their embrace. Instead, in that embrace they set aside their projects in order to attend to each other and give themselves to each other. And then, if a child should happen to result, that child is simply a kind of natural blessing on their love, a gift given them when they were so beside themselves that they could not make or engineer anything. Moreover, the child who is not a product made by them is, then, equal to them in dignity, sharing in their being, and not one whom they have made or whose destiny they should try to determine or control.

Does this really make a difference? Or am I living in a world of pure theory? We should never suppose that ideas lack consequences, and we can reflect on some possible consequences by recalling the relation between responsibility and humility that Michael Sandel elaborated in his widely read *Case against Perfection*. The more reproduction becomes separated from coitus and the more we begin to pick and choose among possible children, the greater the responsibility we shoulder for the character of the next generation. Disposed as we are to believe that being responsible must be a good thing, we may forget that there could be responsibilities that are more godlike than human. As conscientious parents we will, of course, seek to nurture our children on the path toward adulthood. But do we really want to think of ourselves as responsible for shaping not only their nurture but also their nature? Accepting responsibility for the eugenic shaping of our children may smack more of hubris than humility. It may be bad both for us and for them.

A humility that receives children as blessings given us rather than products made by us may deepen our capacity to see in others, whatever their talents or capacities, a dignity equal to our own. After all, we have not made them; we have simply received them as those who mysteriously have a share in our own being. Perhaps, then, a world in which coitus and reproduction have been divorced would not be good for children.

What about sex? Would it be good for sex—that is, for the act of love between a man and a woman? This may seem a little less obvious. Is it good for children? That question seems like a sensible one, however we may happen to answer it. But it may not be as obvious why we should ask my second question. If, however, we rephrase the question in a slightly more traditional way, its significance—and complications—will be apparent. Why continue to think that sexual love and procreation should be held together in the relation of a man and a woman?

Suppose we separate these two in our thought and practice. Sex is one thing—fun, personally fulfilling, potentially relationship-building. Producing children is another—meaningful at least for some, personally fulfilling for many. What happens to the meaning and experience of sex if the two are separated, if the sexual relationship is not in any way oriented toward the next generation? Is it sufficient that sex be fun, a form of play that answers to some deep human needs and desires?

There is no answer to this question likely to meet with universal assent. It may even be—to voice the sort of possibility we are seldom even allowed to consider today—that the answer may to some extent be different for women than for men. In any case, true as it is that sex can be a pleasurable form of play, does thinking of it that way really do justice to the experience—to what sexual partners are seeking from each other? There are countless ways to play, and, on the whole, these are matters for will and choice, personal projects that we take up and continue for as long as they give what we are seeking. But desire is, of course, endless and not easy to satisfy. What even deeply engaging forms of play do not offer is something that is more than just a personal undertaking, something that connects us to deeper—mysterious and mythic—aspects of our humanity. Oriented as it is in its very nature to the next generation, sexual love carries significance that we have not chosen or willed. And perhaps only that sort of significance can justify the kind of vulnerability sex involves, in which a man and woman give (not just their bodies, but) themselves to each other. Perhaps, then—I offer it only as conjecture worth pondering—the divorce of coitus from reproduction, depriving the act of love of the kind of seriousness it traditionally carries, would not be good for sex.

We could simply stop there. But there is an obvious problem left hanging, and we need to consider it. Grant for the sake of argument that it would be bad if we were to create a world in which sex was one thing and reproduction another, with no necessary connection between them. Grant that it would be bad if, as a quite common occurrence, children were produced by non-coital means. Grant that it would be still worse if those means often or regularly had eugenic overtones.

But, then, if reproduction should not be in principle divorced from the sexual relation, should that relation be divorced from reproduction (insofar as it is within our power to do so)? Some questions never go away, and contraception seems to be one of them. If babymaking is best done in the context of lovemaking, as I have been suggesting, may lovemaking deliberately sever its connection to babymaking?

Speaking only for myself, it would be unfortunate if the argument against an autonomous, non-coital world of babymaking should turn out also to be an argument against contraception. Unfortunate in part because in our cultural context it would surely be a losing argument. Nevertheless, arguments that lack cultural purchase are not necessarily false, and that would not in my mind be sufficient reason to give it up. Rather, it would be unfortunate because it would not capture the complexity of marriage as what Paul Ramsey (Fletcher's polar opposite on these matters) called "the covenant of marriage and parenthood."

In marriage the biological and the personal are held together in a union of love. Ramsey argued that this union has its basis not simply in natural law nor, even, in a Christian doctrine of creation. Its deeper basis is the teaching of John's Gospel that God's own creative work was not simply the making of a product but an act of love. Hence, Ramsey believed, "we procreate new beings like ourselves in the midst of our love for one another, and in this there is a trace of the original mystery by which God created the world because of His love." If we think in this way, we will not want a world that separates in principle coitus and reproduction, but this does not mean that we should exercise no control at all in either marriage or parenthood.

Parents are not parents unless they help to shape and direct the course of their children's development. We can and must provide nurture, even if we draw back from the use of techniques aimed at determining our children's nature. Likewise, the exercise of some control over our procreative powers, so long as it does not separate sex from procreation in principle, may have a place in the covenant of marriage and parenthood. To borrow a phrase that I love, even though it failed to gain papal endorsement in *Humanae Vitae*, "the whole ensemble of conjugal acts," though not necessarily each individual act, should be oriented toward procreation. A marriage is not just a collection of individual sexual acts. It is a history—each history unique—in which to learn the meaning of love and care.

None of these judgments can be made with precision, but difficulties and uncertainties do not undermine the central truth that holding together lovemaking and babymaking is good both for children and for sexual love. We do not have to endorse a future world in which coitus and reproduction are routinely separated, as if deep within our humanity the first were not oriented toward the second. We cannot easily discern the direction our culture will take. Perhaps the risks and dangers of reproductive technologies will turn out to be deeply problematic. Perhaps a routine separation of lovemaking from babymaking will turn out to be profoundly unsatisfying. Perhaps we as a society will recoil from parental decisions made on unmistakably eugenic grounds.

And, of course, perhaps none of that will happen. Even so, it will still be true for Christians that in marital love that gives rise to children "there is a trace of the original mystery by which God created the world because of His love." Discerning the implications of that trace and exploring that mystery will not answer perfectly every issue raised for us by reproductive technologies, but it will give us a place from which to take our bearings—a place that will be good for both children and sex.

BIBLIOGRAPHY

Fletcher, Joseph. *The Ethics of Genetic Control: Ending Reproductive Roulette.* Buffalo: Prometheus, 1988.

Ramsey, Paul. *Fabricated Man: The Ethics of Genetic Control.* New Haven: Yale University Press, 1970.

Sandel, Michael J. *The Case against Perfection: Ethics in the Age of Genetic Engineering.* Cambridge: Belknap Press of Harvard University Press, 2007.

6

The End of Sex

Finis or *Telos*?[1]

In a book that deserves serious attention from Christian thinkers, Henry Greely, a professor of law at Stanford University, has made the case for what he calls "the end of sex." Readers may perhaps breathe a sigh of relief when they realize he does not mean that human beings will no longer engage in sexual intercourse for the sheer pleasure of it. What he means is that this pleasure will increasingly be disconnected from the process by which children are conceived.

He predicts that within "the next twenty to forty years" most people who have good health insurance coverage will conceive their children in clinics, using a method he calls "Easy PGD." And in the slightly longer term he can imagine "90 percent of U.S. pregnancies being the result of Easy PGD." Should he turn out to be right about this, at least with respect to relatively wealthy and technologically advanced countries such as the U.S., it will indeed mean an end in one sense—the sense indicated by the Latin word *finis*—to the connection of sexual intercourse and procreation.

---

1. An earlier version of this essay appeared in *Christian Bioethics* 25.2 (August 2019).

That is, our understanding of the two as connected activities will fade. But what about that other sense of "end" signified by the Greek word *telos*? It carries the sense of "purpose." Hence, to say that children are an "end" of sexual intercourse in this sense is to say that one of the purposes of coitus is conception of the next generation of human beings. In that case, to sever this purposive connection would be to lose a significant aspect of our life as sexual beings—the generativity and connection to future generations that fulfill the divine mandate to replenish the earth.

We can think through this issue by examining how Greely anticipates the shift taking place, by considering some of the moral questions he himself thinks it will raise, and by returning finally to consider whether the sort of *finis* to sex that he predicts might not undermine something of great human importance—namely, the *telos* that connects human sexual activity to the birth of children.

POSSIBLE FUTURES

What exactly does Greely mean by Easy PGD? The use of PGD (preimplantation genetic diagnosis) together with in vitro fertilization is already familiar to us and increasingly common in our society. By examining the genetic makeup of embryos that have been produced in the laboratory, physicians can determine which to implant (or, at least, which not to implant). With such assistance prospective parents can avoid giving birth to children with a variety of diseases whose genetic causes are known. Although this does not necessarily make it possible to produce "designer" babies, it does permit would-be parents to select from a range of embryos—at the very least, selecting against certain possibilities and, if they wish, selecting for a boy or a girl.

Greely believes that two technological advances, one already close to a reality, will enable us to move from a relatively limited use of PGD to Easy (and, hence, available for use by many) PGD. The first is our increasing ability to sequence the entire genome and to do so inexpensively. The sequencing can already be done, the cost of doing it has been rapidly dropping, and there is little reason to doubt that it will become affordable for many people in a country such as the United States. To be sure, some technical problems remain. Since the time frame for making decisions about which embryo(s) to implant is short, either interpretation of the sequencing results must be possible within a very short time frame, or embryos must be frozen while the sequencing and interpretation take place. In either case, Greely can see no insuperable obstacles here.

The second—more difficult and as yet unrealized—technological advance needed for Easy PGD is the ability to make eggs in the laboratory, avoiding thereby the costly, burdensome, and dangerous process of egg retrieval from women. If this can be managed, Greely sees no reason why prospective parents could not produce a hundred or more embryos from which to pick and choose one or two for implantation, gestation, and birth. Although he discusses several different techniques that could perhaps be used to produce the needed eggs, Greely thinks that the use of induced pluripotent stem cells (iPSCs) is the most promising and likely. Skin cells taken from people who want to become parents could be "induced" to go backwards, so to speak, differentiating into sperm and eggs that have the genes of those from whom the cells were taken. Greely imagines, reasonably enough, that the fact of genetic connection between the "parent" and the child produced is likely to be especially attractive to many. While this second needed advance has not yet been accomplished, few of us would be likely to bet against its realization in the foreseeable future.

Of course, even with inexpensive genome sequencing and the ability to use iPSCs to produce eggs and sperm, it is always possible that our society might reject such an approach to "making" children. After all, as Greely notes, many in our culture might have reasons strongly to oppose Easy PGD. Supreme Court decisions notwithstanding, a strong prolife movement continues energetically to argue for a view of life that would have no place for a technique that routinely discards embryos. Many Christians in various denominations consider embryos to be babies in their earliest stage of development. And from a quite different perspective, a good many feminists oppose payment for so-called "donation" of eggs for fertilization or payment of surrogates for gestation. Nevertheless, Greely thinks it unlikely that, having put the cup of Easy PGD to our lips, we will not drink it to the bottom—and he may well be right.

From the various reasons he gives in support of this confidence, three strike me as especially determinative. First is the simple fact that the techniques needed for Easy PGD will initially be used to help couples that are infertile. How many in our society will be prepared to oppose that? How many, in particular, of those devout and often conservative religious believers who think of children as a blessing and who are captivated by the desire to have a "child of one's own" will really be prepared to object? And second, this sentimental attachment to a child of one's own will receive more hardheaded support from the fertility services that "make up a large, profitable industry" in this country. This industry "advertises, it lobbies, and it can call on the good will of hundreds of thousands of Americans who are grateful to IVF clinics for giving them 'children of their own.'" Finally, Greely notes that a society which—at least rhetorically—values freedom and eschews government control will have great difficulty getting its government to prohibit any technological advance that is desired by a reasonably large number of citizens.

In short, it will take some very powerful moral arguments to derail the movement toward Easy PGD and prove Greely's predictions mistaken.

MORAL PROBLEMS

Greely's discussion itself points us in the direction of some possible reasons for worrying about or even opposing Easy PGD. In chapter 17 (titled "Just Plain Wrong") he takes up, albeit somewhat halfheartedly, four possible objections. Clearly, he finds them so unpersuasive that he has a hard time taking them seriously and does not really offer much in the way of counterargument. The first such objection is that some of the techniques essential to Easy PGD are contrary to God's will. Those sorts of religious beliefs are, he says, not "attractive," and, besides, different religious traditions have different beliefs, an insight rather too obvious to constitute an argument. On the other hand, when he finds a religious tradition (such as Roman Catholicism) that has clearly developed and authoritative moral arguments on these issues, he simply observes that many Catholics do not adhere to their church's position and that, in any case, it is hard to bring such religious views into public policy arguments. That many Roman Catholic thinkers have addressed this issue (in terms of natural law, for example) does not seem to matter.

A second possible objection is that Easy PGD is unnatural. That claim runs afoul, he thinks, of the naturalistic fallacy, and, he writes, "the problem in the fallacy seems to me to be so self-evident that I will not discuss it any further." It is hard to know how to respond to that, but one feels the need to introduce Greely to folks such as Philippa Foot, Peter Geach, and Alasdair MacIntyre. A third possible reason for thinking Easy PGD would be just plain wrong is the need for humility in the face of the unknown. That, he grants, is an argument for caution. Still, in other areas of life we forge ahead, creating new technologies and changing the world. Why not also in medicine? Perhaps, one might respond, because humility is more than just a reason for caution; it is a virtue that shapes the whole of life. Parenthood, Michael Sandel once noted, "is a school for humility." It teaches us "to be open to the unbidden, . . . a disposition worth affirming not only within families but in the wider world as well." Without such hospitality to the unbidden, our world becomes "a gated community writ large."

Finally, Leon Kass's well-known suggestion that our sense of repugnance in the face of certain actions (such as cloning) points us to a wisdom buried almost too deeply to articulate is a fourth possible ground for objection. This, Greely writes, is a view that he "strongly despise[s]." Moreover, he notes that feelings and emotions change over time; hence, most people in our society may not continue to look on Easy PGD with repugnance. Left unexplained is why despising an argument somehow merits our respect more than experiencing repugnance at certain actions.

All in all, the discussion in chapter 17 is neither careful nor deep. But there are other places, earlier in his discussion, where Greely notes problems that he takes more seriously, and a few of them deserve our consideration.

Easy PGD, because it requires the use of stem cell–derived gametes, would necessarily begin as an experimental procedure. The only way to test its safety would be to use it to produce children—and then see whether they had been harmed in the process. Thus, the children produced would have been experimental subjects who, in the very nature of the case, could not have consented to be used in this way. We can predict that not many researchers will see this as a good reason for refraining from forging ahead in developing the techniques needed for Easy PGD. Indeed, similar arguments were made decades ago when in vitro fertilization was first developed. For example, Paul Ramsey argued forcefully that, morally, we could not even get to know whether it was a safe procedure, for acquiring that knowledge required the use of human subjects (the babies to be produced) who could never volunteer to be used in this way.

As Greely notes, we should not expect similar arguments against Easy PGD to convince large numbers of people to call a halt to continued research. No doubt researchers and bioethicists will settle for obtaining proxy consent from prospective parents, and those would-be parents, in turn, driven by a desire for "a child of their own," will not be hard to persuade. We are entitled to wonder, however, whether all parties involved are not guilty of bad faith. When we consider the enormous attention given in biomedical ethics to the importance—indeed, necessity—of obtaining consent from those who will be research subjects, we might wonder how it is that eagerly hoped for results should be allowed the trump card here. A limit that fades away as the desired goal becomes increasingly possible is not much of a limit.

It is important that we understand this objection properly. It is not an objection that focuses on possible *harms*. Although it is true that children born from IVF may be somewhat more likely to suffer from certain health problems than children naturally conceived, defenders of IVF are entitled to note that the risks are not great. But arguing back and forth about the degree of harm—about which there is, to be sure, much more to be learned—misses the real issue. The point is that human beings who are used without their consent as research subjects have been *wronged*—whether or not they suffer any further harm as a result. If we cannot say this, we are well on our way to undercutting the idea that obtaining consent from research subjects is a fundamental moral requirement that has its ground in the covenant fidelity we owe to others, most especially to the vulnerable. No doubt the researchers, bioethicists, and prospective parents who will approve such research are generally good people eager to produce good results. But that well-intentioned researchers can sometimes do evil should hardly be news in the bioethical world.

Nor is it only the children to be produced who should be the object of our concern. We might also reflect upon the thousands (or more) human embryos who will be used along the way as means to this end. Greely hypothesizes that with Easy PGD prospective parents might produce as many as one hundred embryos from which to pick and choose. When we consider that, even with the comparatively limited use right now of in vitro fertilization, approximately four hundred thousand children are born worldwide each year from IVF, and if we then suppose that countless more people will have recourse to IVF when Easy PGD is available, and if we take seriously the fact that each of them might produce as many as one hundred embryos, the potential number of embryos to be used is staggering.

Each of us began life as just such an embryo, the tiniest and most vulnerable seed of human life. Looked at from this angle we must either give up entirely any sense that human embryos are deserving of at least some respect and protection, or we must grant that Easy PGD, as Greely imagines it, would be a striking case—about as striking as we can imagine—of the strong using the weak for their own purposes. Combining the aims of would-be parents with the multibillion-dollar assisted reproduction industry may produce an exercise in human mastery that largely silences the moral claim of human embryos upon us. And it should make us embarrassed to recall how our public debates in the past have taken seriously assertions that by using only so-called "spare" embryos for research we were demonstrating how seriously we regarded the destruction of embryos.

Another issue worth worrying about is the effect of Easy PGD on people with disabilities—and, surely, there would still be such people, either because their parents had not used Easy PGD or because they had slipped through the cracks of our diagnostic system. Greely recounts a conference on noninvasive prenatal testing at which one panelist was a young woman who was largely confined to a wheelchair because of spinal muscular atrophy. During a break in the conference, she said to him, "If you had your way, I would not have been born." "That," he writes, "rocked me." He seems, however, to have recovered nicely. Still, there is valid reason for concern. I do not know whether a world in which Easy PGD was widely used would be one in which people with disabilities might subtly be invited to suppose it would be better if they did not exist at all, but one can certainly imagine that some might be tempted to feel that way. At the very least, it is not at all hard to believe that in such a world there would be less urgency to seek new treatments for their disabilities. The favored many might be less inclined to spend resources on conditions affecting relatively few. Nor is it hard to believe that some of us—and, certainly, some insurance companies or a financially strapped government health care payer—might feel that parents who had declined to use Easy PGD would just have to live with the consequences of their choice.

FINIS OR TELOS?

Serious as these concerns about Easy PGD are, even they do not, in my view, penetrate to the deepest reason Christians have for concern about a future marked by widespread use of Easy PGD. The fundamental problem is that the sort of *finis* to sex that Greely foresees will undermine the *telos* given in creation that connects human sexual activity to the birth of children.

Our experience of ourselves as embodied is, as Roger Scruton has observed, "incipiently dualistic." Sometimes I experience myself as embodied—personally present in the body and its actions. But I may also experience myself as in some way distanced from my body—*having* my body rather than *being* that body. And these experiences may happen simultaneously. Thus, for example, falling from a great height I may know my*self* as a falling object even while there are aspects of my subjective experience that cannot be captured by a formula about the mass and velocity of falling objects. I both am and am not that falling object. When we reflect upon involuntary bodily responses such as blushing, smiling, crying, or having an erection we get some sense of what it could mean to say that we are "incarnate person[s]."

Perhaps nowhere is this truth about human beings more evident than in our sexual experience. On the one hand, that experience is rooted in biology and ordered toward reproduction of the species. But on the other hand, we know implicitly that it is not just an animal act. It is also deeply personal, a giving of one*self* in the body. This suggests that, in order to do justice to the two-sidedness of our humanity, reproduction should not be simply an act of technical manufacture in which, distancing ourselves from the body, we use the body to produce a child. Rather, reproduction becomes a characteristically human act when it is the fruit of mutual, embodied self-giving in love.

In fact, once we begin to think this way, we will see that the sexual act so understood is not even adequately characterized as "reproduction." To be sure, the sexual act between a man and a woman is naturally ordered toward the birth of children. That much is biological fact. But in the act itself the man and woman are not simply using their bodies to produce a desired result. They are giving themselves—ecstatically stepping out of themselves—in search of oneness in love. Should a child be conceived as a result, that child is not simply a product of their technical capacity to use their bodies to achieve desired aims. On the contrary, that child is the gift bestowed upon their mutual self-giving. Contrast this with Greely's characterization: "The process of human reproduction is wasteful, expensive, and bizarrely complicated. Such a process surely must be the product of evolution, because no one would have designed it this way. . . . Ultimately, this book is about the ways we are likely to redesign that system, to make it less wasteful, expensive, and complicated." We see here the difference between an act governed by the rational will of persons who use their bodies to achieve a desired result and an act of interpersonal love between incarnate persons.

Thus, built into our human lovemaking is a *telos* we have not ourselves given to it or chosen. Sometimes, though not of course always or inevitably, lovemaking results in a child, demonstrating thereby that it is truly procreation. Hence, although if with Greely we think of human beings as rational agents using their sexual organs to achieve desired results, the process of human reproduction seems "wasteful, expensive, and bizarrely complicated," it looks quite different when we do not distance ourselves in this way from our bodies. The birth of a child then is seen not as a goal external to the sexual act but as its internal fruition—its *telos*, even if not its only *telos*.

I pause here for a moment to make clear what I do not mean. Obviously, my depiction of the significance of the sexual act has similarities to Roman Catholic teaching regarding the unitive and procreative purposes of marriage. In affirming that these are not to be separated, Roman Catholicism surely intends to understand procreation as a *telos* of sexual intercourse. It does not want to think of the sexual act as one thing and the conception of a child as something entirely external to it. But in teaching that each and every conjugal act, in order to be a true conjugal act, must refrain from willed contraception (apart, of course, from natural family planning), the church's teaching seems to go well beyond understanding the possible conception of a child as a *telos* of the act. In fact, on the Roman Catholic view intercourse that uses contraception cannot be the sexual act in its full sense. What a strange result! For it turns out that the church's teaching focuses on biological reproduction every bit as much as does Greely. He does so in order to rationalize the process of reproduction, separating it entirely from lovemaking. Traditional church teaching does it in order to characterize contraceptive intercourse as something less than an act of mutual love in the full sense. This hardly does justice to the unitive significance of the act of love.

The shared history that a husband and wife promise in the marriage vow is more than a series of separate, isolated acts of sexual intercourse. That is, they are not engaging in a series of one-night stands. The vow they take binds together their lives over time, and it is the whole of their time together that should, if God so blesses them, prove fruitful. It is better, therefore, to hold that the love-giving sexual union of a husband and wife should hope to be life-giving, not necessarily in each and every sexual act but in the whole ensemble of those acts. Then children born to them will still be a gift bestowed on them—a true *telos* of their marital life—and not just the result of a reproductive project they have undertaken.

In order to understand why we should draw back from producing children in the laboratory—whether by IVF and PGD as currently used or by the Easy version Greely envisions—our most important task is not to criticize the process of Easy PGD. Rather, we should remind ourselves why it is humanly significant to hold together procreation of children and the bond of sexual love between a man and woman.

From one angle, doing so enriches the relation of husband and wife. Understanding that a child is the possible fruit of their lovemaking, seeing conception of a child as a *telos* of their mutual self-giving, can free them from a certain kind of self-absorption. They are not encouraged to suppose that the *telos* of their love is always and only their own pleasure or self-fulfillment. So narrow a world lacks spaciousness. Its lovers only turn inward to face each other, but never—in their oneness—outward to the world. But so long as they genuinely hope that their acts of love, taken as a whole, will be fruitful, then, even if their love does not or cannot give rise to children, they can understand that love as their participation in a form of life that carries its own inner meaning, having a *telos* established in the creation, and not just their private search for meaning or fulfillment. To write *finis* over sexual love as procreative and to lose the *telos* that connects that love to the next generation would make the sexual act between a man and a woman what Oliver O'Donovan has called "simply a profound form of play." However enticing this may sound to us in certain moods or moments, its narrowness is as likely to result in the death as in the enrichment of love.

Looking from a second angle, we may suspect that being conceived and born in the old-fashioned way may be better for children than being produced in a laboratory (whether by Easy PGD or more primitive methods). Consider what it means to think of a child as the fruit of sexual lovemaking. It means that a man and woman, setting aside their personal projects and stepping ecstatically outside themselves in order to give themselves to each other, have been blessed with a gift they have not made. And if we understand our children as gifts and blessings, not products that are the work of our hands, we can hardly suppose it is our role or right to determine their destiny or judge the worth of their lives. We will have to think of them as our equals, created not by us but by the same hand—God or Nature—to whom we owe our own existence. No child will have to say to his parents what that young, disabled woman said to Greely: "If you had your way, I would not have been born." And, of course, to see this is to see why all use of PGD is morally questionable, and why a world in which it became easy and commonplace would be a world in which affirmation of human equality would be mere lip service.

The degree to which Easy PGD might in principle encourage us to think of children as products manufactured to suit our desires becomes clear when Greely discusses some of the most far-reaching of its possible results. If the advances he predicts are achieved, it could be possible to produce what he calls "cross-sex" gametes. That is, using iPSCs we could perhaps make sperm from a woman's cells or ova from a man's cells (though he thinks the first of these will be more difficult than the second). If this can be done, we can then imagine a future "uniparent." A child could be produced using sperm and egg derived from cells of the same person. Here we see the culmination of the narrowness and lack of spaciousness that characterizes laboratory reproduction more generally. Producing a child in this way would clearly be an individual project undertaken to satisfy one's own desires, not a gift bestowed upon shared love. Perhaps the best we can hope for in such circumstances is that the *telos* inscribed in our nature will reassert itself through rebellion of the child against its manufacturer. Of course, this most far-reaching possibility of Easy PGD—the uniparent— may prove impossible to achieve, but the fact that Greely can consider it should move us to realize that something has gone wrong with the project from the outset.

Finally, one further point should not escape our attention. Critics of the view I have developed here are likely to suggest that to think of children as a *telos* of the sexual act is to import metaphysical assumptions—no doubt, in our society, Christian ones—into the discussion. While granting that one is entitled—privately—to hold such beliefs if one wishes, they will argue that these beliefs are out of place in discussions of what our public policy with respect to Easy PGD or assisted reproduction more generally should be.

There is a good bit of self-deception in such a claim, and we should not treat it as if it were weighty or profound. For the vision of human re-production that would undergird a world of Easy PGD comes encumbered with its own metaphysical baggage. As Paul Ramsey noted years ago, when we dismember procreation into its several parts and then combine them in new and different ways, we simply depict a new myth of creation in which human beings are created with two separate faculties—one that expresses the union of partners through sexual relations, and another that produces children by means of "a cool, deliberate act of man's rational will." That is to say, when thinking about matters as significant as human sexual love and the birth of children, we cannot free ourselves of metaphysical or religious baggage. Nor should we want to. For to turn away from a world of Easy PGD in which children are a means to satisfying our projects and desires, and to turn back to a world in which children are welcomed as a blessing bestowed upon our mutual self-giving in love, is to realize and affirm, in Gabriel Marcel's words, that "the truest fidelity is creative."

BIBLIOGRAPHY

Greely, Henry T. *The End of Sex and the Future of Human Reproduction*. Cambridge: Harvard University Press, 2016.

Marcel, Gabriel. *Homo Viator: Introduction to a Metaphysic of Hope*. New York: Harper Torchbooks, 1962.

O'Donovan, Oliver. *Begotten or Made? Human Procreation and Medical Technique*. Oxford: Clarendon, 1984.

Ramsey, Paul. *Fabricated Man: The Ethics of Genetic Control*. New Haven: Yale University Press, 1970.

Sandel, Michael J. *The Case against Perfection: Ethics in the Age of Genetic Engineering*. Cambridge: Belknap Press of Harvard University Press, 2007.

Scruton, Roger. *Sexual Desire: A Moral Philosophy of the Erotic*. New York: Free Press, 1986.

7

Designing Our Descendants[1]

In one of the classic early discussions of possible uses of advancing genetic knowledge to control and reshape human life, Paul Ramsey, more than thirty years ago, wrote the following:

> I may pause here to raise the question whether a scientist has not an entirely "frivolous conscience" who, faced with the awesome technical possibility that soon human life may be created in the laboratory and then be either terminated or preserved in existence as an experiment, or, who gets up at scientific meetings and gathers to himself newspaper headlines by urging his colleagues to prepare for that scientific accomplishment by giving attention to the "ethical" questions it raises—if he is not at the same time, and in advance, prepared to stop the whole procedure should the "ethical finding" concerning this fact-situation turn out to be, for any serious conscience, murder. It would perhaps be better not to raise the ethical issues, than not to raise them in earnest.

My aim here is to invite thought about *present* uses of genetic screening and the attitude we ought *now* to have toward the project of shaping our children, lest a focus on *future* possibilities tempt us here and now to "an entirely 'frivolous conscience.'"

1. An earlier version of this essay appeared in *First Things* 109 (January 2001).

No one doubts that genetic advance will, in good time, enable us to find therapies for at least some of the devastating diseases whose causes are, in whole or part, genetic. Research is taking place on many different fronts. Xeno-transplantation—that is, transplantation of animal organs, probably pig organs, into human beings—is explored as a possible answer to the organ shortage. Genetic therapy—in which a functioning copy of a gene is added, or, even more desirable were it possible, a defective gene is removed and replaced with a functioning version—is the holy grail of research. Although progress on the therapeutic front has been slower than many had predicted, it remains the focus of much research and many hopes, and the recent development of a method of gene "editing" called CRISPR/Cas9 has made future success more likely. Perhaps more dramatically still, what is called germline therapy—an alteration not of the somatic cells of the body but of the germ cells, the sex cells by which traits are passed on to future generations—is increasingly defended and may become possible. Just as striking is the work being done to culture embryonic stem cells in order to grow organs or tissues for transplant. Because such stem cells are essentially immortal—they simply regenerate themselves—this research may even hold out the hope of retarding the aging process, which some people, at least, think desirable.

In short, from countless different angles the pace of research invites us to reflect upon the project of controlling and reshaping human beings or, more broadly still, human nature—all in the name of relieving suffering and extending life. Our language regularly invites us to view this project in favorable terms. Consider, for example, the verbal formulations I might have used here. I might have said that researchers are "progressing" or "advancing" in the treatment of genetic disease and applications of molecular biology in medicine. It would have been surprising and counterintuitive had I written that the sorts of possibilities mentioned above indicate that researchers are "regressing" or "retreating." We can scarcely imagine that increased ability to relieve suffering or eliminate defect and disease could be anything other than progress and advance. At the same time, everyone also acknowledges that new techniques could be misused, even though few agree on exactly what would constitute such misuse. So, for example, we have distinguished between somatic cell and germ cell therapy, often approving the former and disapproving the latter. But anyone reading the literature will surely note how that line has begun to break down of late, as an increasing number of bioethicists seem willing to defend germline interventions. Or, we have drawn a line between therapy and enhance-ment—embracing the former while disapproving the latter. But, again, any-one reading the literature will note how this line too has begun to blur. In response to that blurring we may try to distinguish between health-related and non-health-related enhancements—between, for example, enhancing the body's ability to fight certain cancers and enhancing memory or, even, kindness—but it would surely be naive of us to suppose that the pressure to blur this line will not also be enormous.

WHAT KIND OF PEOPLE ARE WE?

To the degree that we as a people have lost the capacity to draw lines, to decide what should and should not be done, we are forced to take refuge in virtue ethics. That is, if we cannot definitively say which acts should or should not be done, perhaps we can trust people of good character to use these new techniques without abusing them. Yet, of course, *we* are the people who will be using the advances in genetics and whose wisdom and virtue must be trusted. What kind of people are we? To answer that ques-tion we need to think not about what may be possible in the future but, rather, about what is done in the present. We need to focus not on future subjunctives but on present indicatives.

And our present condition is this: We have entered a new era of eugenics. That science which attempts to improve the inherited charac-teristics of the species and which had gone so suddenly out of fashion after World War II and the Nazi doctors now climbs steadily back toward respectability. Eugenics becomes respectable again insofar as it promises to relieve suffering, as it claims for itself the virtue of compassion. The new eugenics has, however, a distinctly postmodern ring. In the heyday of eugenics early in the twentieth century, its proponents had in mind government-sponsored programs that might even involve centralized co-ercion (and, of course, the Nazi program of eliminating the unfit certainly warranted such a description). Thus, for example, "A Geneticists's Mani-festo," signed in 1939 by twenty-two very eminent American and British scientists, called for replacement of the "superstitious attitude towards sex and reproduction now prevalent" with "a scientific and social attitude" that would make it "an honor and a privilege, if not a duty, for a mother, married or unmarried, or for a couple, to have the best children possible, both in respect of their upbringing and their genetic endowment."

By contrast, the new eugenics comes embedded in the language of privacy and choice. Its two cardinal virtues—almost the only virtues our culture now knows—are compassion and consent. Compassion moves us to relieve suffering whenever possible; consent requires that our compassion be "privatized." A world in which prenatal screening followed by abortion of children diagnosed with defects has become a routine part of medical care for pregnant women—that is to say, our world—is one into which eugenics enters not through government programs but precisely as government removes itself from what is seen as entirely a private choice.

I am not invoking the "Nazi analogy," which has been disputed as often as it has been invoked in bioethical argument. I am not claiming that we find ourselves on a slippery slope, at the foot of which might lie Nazi-like deeds. Instead, I simply note how easily we may deceive ourselves about what we do here and now, how subjectively well-meaning people may approve objective evil. Just that, in fact, is the most terrifying point of Robert Jay Lifton's great work, *The Nazi Doctors*. He invites us to see within ourselves—good people whom we suppose ourselves to be—the possibility of great evil. "We thus find ourselves returning," Lifton writes near the end of his discussion of the "doubling" that made it psychologically possible to be a Nazi doctor, "to the recognition that most of what Nazi doctors did would be within the potential capability—at least under certain conditions—of most doctors and of most people." To read Lifton's account is, for the most part, to read of ordinary people in the grip of an ideology, who suppose themselves to be engaged in a compassionate and healing endeavor. Something like that, Lifton suggests, is an almost universal possibility. And something like that, I am suggesting—something very different because cloaked in the language of privacy, yet not so different because it sanitizes and medicalizes as healing the killing of "defectives"—is by far the most common present use of genetic "advance."

This is our present situation. The day may come when we can treat and cure prenatally or postnatally many genetic diseases; however, for the moment we can diagnose prenatally far more than we can treat. In the meantime, therefore, we screen and abort. For now, that is almost the only "treatment" for illness diagnosed prenatally. We know more and more about the child *in utero*; hence, people quite naturally seek and use such knowledge in order to select the babies they desire and abort those they do not want. This is the new eugenics—which relies not on government coercion but on private choice and desire, on the commodification of children.

Thus, Bryan Appleyard notes, "we could not now respectably speak of 'the improvement of the race' or of 'selective breeding'—the terminology of the old eugenics—but we do speak of the 'quality of life' and assess our children in consumerist terms." Not only is the meaning of childhood distorted but the meaning of parenthood as well. Selective abortion means selective acceptance. The unconditional character of maternal and paternal love is replaced by choice, quality control, and conditional acceptance.

People who have chosen or have been taught to think this way are the people who will be deciding what constitutes proper use or misuse of advancing genetic technology. We run the risk of cultivating frivolous consciences, therefore, if we pay attention to the moral conundrums of future subjunctives while studiously ignoring present indicatives. For as long as we are willing to rely on the routinized practice of prenatal screening followed by selective abortion we are not people who should be trusted to design their descendants.

WHAT KIND OF DESCENDANTS SHOULD WE WANT?

Suppose, however, that we could be so trusted and that the capacity to design and shape our children, to shape their nature and character, were really ours, what sort of people should we aim to create? Taking my inspiration from a short piece written by Alasdair MacIntyre more than four decades ago, I suggest that we ponder this question briefly. An obvious way to answer the question is to think in terms that our moral tradition has taught us, in terms of the four cardinal and the three theological virtues. We should aim to design children who would be characterized by prudence, justice, courage, and temperance—and, in addition, by faith, hope, and love.

Within the Western moral tradition, the virtue of prudence means something quite different from our use today of a word such as *prudential*. For us, in fact, there is a certain tension between being good and being prudent. In the longer view of the tradition, however, the virtue of prudence enables us to see things as they really are. Not just as we would like them to be, or fear that they must be, or greedily hope they may be— but as they truly are.

Two things follow. On the one hand, this implies that nature herself— apart from our own shaping activity—has order and form to be discerned by the prudent man or woman. Prudence seeks to conform to the reality of things and does not suppose that our humanity consists only in our power of mastery over nature. Hence, the first task is not to change the world but to understand and interpret it. On the other hand, human prudence can never exhaust or comprehensively understand the meaning and order of our world. MacIntrye notes that the limits to our understanding are evident in the very possibility of radical conceptual innovation. Relying on Karl Popper, he asks what it would have been like had one of our ancestors predicted the invention of the wheel. In order to explain his prediction this ancestor would have had to describe axle, rim, and spokes—in short, not just to predict the invention of but, in fact, to invent the wheel. The lesson being this: we simply cannot predict with any precision what the future may be like, what innovations may appear, and we will want children who can accept the limits of our knowledge, who know that not everything is within our control.

To see the world rightly is, among other things, to see the difference between "mine" and "thine"—that is, to be just. Justice is not yet love; it is life *with*, not life *for*, the neighbor. Without denying our fellow humanity, justice maintains distance between us, lest the life of one should be entirely absorbed within the aims and purposes of another. Hence, to be just is to respect the rights of others, to recognize the claim upon us of their equal dignity. The denial of that common humanity is, as Josef Pieper writes, "the formal justification for every exercise of totalitarian power." Such power, of course, can be exercised not only synchronically but also diachronically—across generations.

Justice requires, at least in some times and places, courage. For there will be moments when it is injurious to one's own interests or, simply, dangerous to be just. Courage is a necessary human virtue precisely because we are creatures always vulnerable to injury—the greatest of which is, of course, death. We have tended to picture courage as a martial virtue needed by those who must face enemies and fight. But in our world, and perhaps in any world, it is needed as much by those who only suffer—not those who attack, but those who endure. It is needed if we are, one day, to accept the appropriateness of our own death, to acknowledge that a just affirmation of the claims of others means that we must recognize that our own time and place is not the master of every time and place, that we must give place to those who come after us.

To be that courageous in the service of justice cannot be possible for one whose inner self is not fundamentally in right order and at peace. Lacking such order, we are bound to grasp for what we desire at any moment, to flinch when sacrifice of our own desires seems needed for the sake of others. We should, therefore, want our children to be not only prudent, just, and courageous, but also temperate.

High as such an ideal of character is, however, Christians will not rest content with an ideal that can be and has been known apart from Christ. They will also want the threefold graces of faith, hope, and love to be formed in their children. Faith is, as the New Testament Letter to the Hebrews puts it, "the conviction of things not seen." Because we cannot fully see the way ahead, because, as I noted above, we must always live with uncertainty about the future, we are unable to secure our own lives. We exercise control of various sorts, we improve the human condition, but mastery eludes us. Hence, we must want our children to know the limits of their power, to seek wisdom more than power. Indeed, if our faith seeks its security finally in God, our life must be oriented toward One who most emphatically is not within our control. As Robert Meagher writes, describing St. Augustine's view, "It seems that one may either strive to want the right thing, or strive to have what one wants. The search for wisdom somehow involves the re-nunciation of power, the renunciation of possession, while the search for power somehow involves the renunciation of wisdom, since it presupposes the appropriateness of what it is striving to attain."

Because faith requires that we live without trying to secure our own future, it needs to be joined with the virtue of hope. We must hope and expect that God can complete what is incomplete in our own strivings, especially when, in order to live justly, we refrain from achieving good that can be gotten only by evil means. "You might have helped me," future generations may say, "had you only been willing to dirty your hands a bit." There is no reply to such a charge without an appeal to hope, without a sense of the limits of our responsibility to do the good. "Above all," Kierkegaard writes, "the one who in truth wills the Good must not be 'busy.' In quiet patience he must leave it to the Good itself, what reward he shall have, and what he shall accomplish." To be hopeful is to adopt the posture of one who waits, who knows his fundamental neediness and dependence; for, after all, were the good for which we wait at our own disposal, there would be no need for hope.

There remains love, the greatest of the virtues. Love signifies approval. Hence, our own love should mirror the creative love of God, which bestows on us the divine word of approval. Love therefore is, in Josef Pieper's words, a way of turning to another and saying, "It's good that you exist; it's good that you are in this world." As we hope to become people who can love our own children in this way, so we would want them, in turn, to be people who can love as they have been loved—with an affirmation that is not conditioned upon the qualities of the loved one.

We can say, by way of summary, that were we to undertake the project of designing our descendants, we should want them to be people who do not think the natural world infinitely malleable to their projects; who reckon from the outset with limits to their own knowledge of and control over the future; who respect the equal dignity of their fellows and do not seek to co-opt others as means to their own (even if good) ends; who acknowledge their own death, the ultimate of limits; who are prepared to subordinate their needs to the good of others; who are more disposed to seek wisdom than power; who know that the good is not finally at their own disposal; and who live in a manner that says to others, "It's good that you exist."

My discussion has come at the question of designing our descendants in two stages. I first suggested that people who live as we do—who have accepted as useful the routinized practice of prenatal screening—are people who have no business attempting to reach out and shape future generations. But, second, I asked what kind of descendants we should seek to create if we were people fit to undertake such a task. If we are drawn to the description I have given in terms of the cardinal and the theological virtues, we should be able to see, from a quite different angle, why designing descendants is a project we ought not to undertake. I said earlier that I took the inspiration for this idea from Alasdair MacIntyre, and I can do no better than repeat here the words with which he concluded his own exploration of the traits we should want our children to have:

> If in designing our descendants we succeeded in designing people who possessed just those traits that I have described, . . . [w]hat we would have done is to design descendants whose virtues would be such that they would be quite unwilling in turn to design *their* descendants. We should in fact have brought our own project of designing descendants to an end.

Better, it would seem, never to have set foot on this path.

BIBLIOGRAPHY

Appleyard, Bryan. *Brave New Worlds: Staying Human in the Genetic Future*. New York: Viking, 1998.

Lifton, Robert Jay. *The Nazi Doctors*. New York: Basic Books, 1986.

MacIntyre, Alasdair. "Seven Traits for the Future." *The Hastings Center Report* 9 (1970) 5–7.

Pieper, Josef. *The Four Cardinal Virtues: Prudence, Justice, Fortitude, Temperance*. Notre Dame: University of Notre Dame Press, 1966.

Ramsey, Paul. *Fabricated Man: The Ethics of Genetic Control*. New Haven: Yale University Press, 1970.

8

A Yellow Light for Gene Editing[1]

Several of my children, in the summer before they began kindergarten, participated in a program called "Safety City." Among the ditties that seems destined to stick in my head forever is one they learned there:

> The traffic light you see ahead
> is sometimes green and sometimes red.
> The red on top means "stop, stop, stop."
> The green below means "go, go, go."

Noticeably missing from this little piece of poetic instruction is the yellow light. Perhaps one has to be a little older to learn how to deal with it. We're supposed to stop when the yellow light falls, but sometimes we're already quite near the intersection. So then we tend to treat it like a warning sign and just "proceed with caution."

I'm pretty sure I never thought much about the yellow light until I learned to drive. In the early stages of my driving experience I heeded it religiously. I never entered an intersection on a yellow light. I think I even slowed just slightly (a bad idea, actually) as I approached an intersection, just in case the yellow light should suddenly appear. My approach was to proceed *with caution*.

---

1. An earlier version of this essay appeared under the title "Is Caution Enough?" in *Commonweal* 144.7 (April 14, 2017)

Those days are gone. Now I mostly just *proceed*. Not only do I routinely enter intersections when the traffic light is yellow, I am likely to accelerate a bit as I approach, the better to proceed before the red light drops. To be sure, I do not run red lights. But over time, as life's routines have accustomed me to intersections, the yellow has become less and less distinguishable from the green, even though in theory I am supposed to stop for it. And I suspect that my experience is not all that uncommon. Knowing that I don't run red lights, I have a pretty good conscience about sailing through on the yellow.

I found myself thinking about yellow lights as I looked through the exhaustively detailed report *Human Genome Editing: Science, Ethics, and Governance*, released in 2017 by an advisory group formed by the National Academy of Sciences and the National Academy of Medicine. In most ways the salient moral issues do not seem to me to have changed much from the last time I thought at length about these issues roughly a decade earlier.

One thing, however, has changed considerably: namely, the development of what is called CRISPR/Cas9, a new method for "editing" the human genome. Attempts at gene therapy, although not terribly successful, have been around for some time. What CRISPR/Cas9 appears to offer, however, is an efficient and precise method for altering (both by addition and deletion) an organism's genetic material. We stand on the brink of an age in which our capacity to modify the human genome may increase enormously. And not surprisingly scientists are eager to proceed with gene-editing research.

What sorts of research are under consideration or, at least, possible? Most obviously, basic laboratory research that does not, at least for now, attempt clinical applications. In addition to increasing our understanding of human biology generally, such research could increase our understanding of important areas of medicine, positioning us for future attempts at clinical applications. Researchers could increase their understanding of fertility and reproduction, perhaps opening doors for greater success with in vitro fertilization (IVF) and related techniques. They might create disease models for study, with the hope of one day developing new approaches to treatment.

Still more dramatically—and the issue that received the most notice in news stories about the academies' report—researchers might develop further the capacity to do what the report calls "heritable germline editing." Most cells in the body are known as somatic cells (from the Greek word *soma*, meaning "body"). These cells are differentiated to form the body's organs, tissues, skin, and bones. Somatic cells may undergo change (through mutation, for instance), but those changes die when the individual dies. They are not passed on to future generations. By contrast, germ cells, which give rise to sperm and eggs, are not differentiated into the various parts of the body, and changes in the germline could be inherited by future generations. Hence, to "edit" the germline is to exercise power over not just a single individual patient but also over descendants of that individual into an indefinite future.

In principle, somatic cell research aimed at developing possible treatments for disease is not controversial. It is simply an extension of medicine's attempt to treat patients—to cure or ameliorate disease and debilitating injury. Genetic therapies might one day enable us to treat inherited genetic diseases such as cystic fibrosis or Tay-Sachs. Research in what is called regenerative medicine may increase our capacity to help those suffering from Parkinson's or Alzheimer's, or to produce sheets of skin for burn victims, or to replace heart muscle. To be sure, many things can go awry—and sometimes have—when we proceed from somatic cell research to clinical attempts at genetic therapy. But at least for any work supported by federal government funding, we have in place a number of regulatory mechanisms aimed at ensuring, as much as possible, that attempts at genetic therapy will take place only after their safety has been rigorously studied and we have reason to believe the hoped-for benefits of the therapy are greater than its risks. In general, the report of the academies regards this current regulatory structure as adequate for somatic cell research, and there seems little reason to disagree.

The possibility of increasingly powerful and precise editing of germ cells raises more complicated moral questions of several different sorts. Why, apart from a general desire to expand the frontiers of our knowledge, might anyone want to do it? One reason is that heritable genome editing could, as the report puts it, "be the only or most acceptable option for prospective parents who wish to have a genetically related child while minimizing the risk of transmitting a serious disease or disability." There are, of course, other ways to try to reach the same end, though I hardly wish to recommend most of them. We could use prenatal genetic diagnosis (PGD) of a fetus in utero and selectively abort any fetuses with genetic disease. Or we could use PGD of embryos in the laboratory, selecting only those embryos free of genetic disease for implantation through IVF. Still other alternatives exist. Prospective parents might use donated gametes; they might adopt children;

or they might decide, given the risk that they may transmit genetic disease, not to have children. "These options, however," the report notes, "do not allow both parents to have a genetic connection to their children, which is of great importance to many people."

Before turning to other important moral issues raised by the possibility of germ cell editing, it is—at least for Christians—worth thinking briefly about this seeming importance of genetic connection. The British theologian and ethicist Michael Banner has noted that, despite the seeming gulf between their views, advocates of IVF and Roman Catholic critics of those techniques almost try to "outbid" each other in expressing "profound respect for biological parenthood." To be sure, the former do it in order to help infertile couples produce "a child of their own," the latter in order to reject techniques of assisted reproduction. But Banner invites us to consider whether this may not be "a relatively minor disagreement between parties which share very similar understandings of the relationship between parent and child." If he perhaps slightly overstates the case, it is nonetheless true that both views leave the rather fervent desire for a genetic connection between parents and children "solemnly in place on its contemporary pedestal." Unless we break the power of that desire, I suspect that we will be unable to resist what will almost surely seem to be (as the report notes) a promising way to have genetically related children without passing on to those children a serious disease.

More generally, what should we think about germline editing, which "in the not so distant future" may, the report concludes, "become a realistic possibility"? Were it not so important, I would be tempted to characterize the central moral issue here as "intriguing" or "fascinating." On the one hand, editing germ cells to eliminate serious disease has the potential to prevent suffering not only for a single individual but also for that person's descendants. It eliminates the need for continued interventions at the somatic level for each new generation. On the other hand, that potential good is exactly the problem: germline editing may eliminate disease not only for a single individual but also for that person's descendants. That is to say, whereas somatic cell genetic therapy is simply an extension of what medicine has always sought to do, we might wonder whether germ cell editing should even be characterized as medicine. The "patient" is no longer a particular suffering human being; instead, the object of such proposed interventions is what Paul Ramsey once called "that celebrated nonpatient, the human species." The possibility of unforeseen and unintended consequences is considerable, and it is not silly to wonder whether human beings—ourselves included—should ever seek to exercise this kind of control over those who will come after us. Recognizing such concerns, the report says, "Heritable germline editing trials must be approached with caution, but caution does not mean that they must be prohibited." Which is to say, it sets before us a yellow light.

Inevitably, germline research raises another issue that has dogged our public discourse since the topic of stem cell research became important several decades ago—namely, the use and destruction of human embryos. In some ways the report simply does not engage the moral issue, saying, "This report does not address those ethical arguments, and accepts as given the current legal and regulatory policies that apply in each country."

Nevertheless, there are peculiarities in the report worth noting. Describing the various approaches taken in different countries, it says, "Views on the legal and moral status of the human embryo range from treating it the same as any other human tissue, to considering it a tissue deserving of some extra degree of respect, to viewing it as tissue that should be accorded the same respect or even the same legal rights as a live-born child." What a peculiar formulation that is! I would think that those who believe a human embryo should have respect equal to that of a live-born child are likely to describe that embryo not as tissue but as one of us—a living human being in the earliest stages of its development, having the characteristics we all did at that stage of life.

There are also strange juxtapositions scattered throughout the report. At a number of places it notes that any research that destroys embryos or creates them solely for use in research may not be funded by the federal government's Department of Health and Human Services. This is due to a provision known as the Dickey-Wicker Amendment that has been attached to the Health and Human Services appropriations bill every year since 1996. (The research can, of course, be funded by other sources, except in some states where it is illegal.) Yet, without ever recommending a change in this funding policy, the report just as often expresses a relentless pressure to proceed, to move forward with research that would involve the destruction of embryos. So, for example, shortly after noting the federal refusal to fund that has been in place for two decades, it states, "Important scientific and clinical issues relevant to human fertility and reproduction require continued laboratory research on human gametes and their progenitors, human embryos and pluripotent stem cells. This research is necessary for medical and scientific purposes that are not directed at heritable genome editing, though it will also provide valuable information and techniques that could be applied if heritable genome editing were to be attempted in the future." Elsewhere it describes recommendations of a 1994 NIH Human Embryo Research Panel as "recognized within the scientific community as a more general evaluation of the ethics and acceptability of such research." Those recommendations supported federal funding for research on embryos and (in some circumstances when deemed "necessary" to attain important scientific knowledge) the creation of embryos for use in research. It is worth recalling, however, that Congress rejected the funding recommendation of that panel and President Clinton specifically withdrew from consideration for funding any research that created embryos simply for use in research.

At any rate, the effect of these juxtapositions is to exert a constant pressure to proceed with research that U.S. government authorities are unable even to consider supporting at the present time. Acknowledging the restrictions in place while asserting the necessity of the research has the effect of making the restrictions seem irrational. Insofar as that is the overall effect, it is not quite accurate to think of the report as prescinding from the moral and legal arguments. Via the claim of medical necessity it presses for expanded, though always regulated, research that uses embryos. And it is worth reminding ourselves that we are not talking about research that might use just a few embryos—some very limited exception. What is deemed necessary is the use of countless embryos—always, of course, with caution and with relief of suffering as the ultimate end in view.

There remains one further possibility on the gene-editing horizon. Beyond basic research or somatic cell editing, beyond even heritable genome editing, there is the possibility of "enhancing" our traits and capacities. This is, as the report rightly notes, a notoriously difficult concept to define. We all understand in general that the idea has something to do with improving a trait beyond its typical level, moving beyond what is simply therapeutic, but it can be hard to be more precise than that. Moreover, it is quite possible that a product may have dual uses, some clearly therapeutic, others more like enhancement. So a treatment designed to maintain muscle mass in the elderly may also help to improve the capacities of wrestlers. Given these complexities, and given that a technique such as CRISPR/Cas9 is still in early stages of development, the report draws back somewhat, encouraging a focus "at this time" on therapy rather than enhancement:

"Regulatory agencies should not at this time authorize clinical trials of somatic or germline genome editing for purposes other than treatment or prevention of disease or disability." Reasonable as this no doubt seems and probably is, one might wish the report had probed some of the deeper philosophical questions a bit more. Are there research aims that, however well intentioned, would seek to bestow traits of character and skills that have no value apart from the process by which they are developed and achieved? Might the drive to enhance human capacities cause us to lose a sense of the "giftedness" of human life, making us, in Michael Sandel's nice phrase, "inhospitable to the unbidden"? Perhaps these are not the sorts of questions we should ask a committee of the National Academies to address. Fair enough. But then we also need to acknowledge that there are limits to how instructive such a report can be.

Finally, I return to where I began: the meaning of a yellow light. On the whole, this report on human genome editing seems to me to set before us a yellow light, which should invite us to think about how we actually treat yellow lights. Surely they are useful. We recognize that it would be foolhardy for us just to forge ahead without taking due care to avoid possible unforeseen harms; hence, no green light. But at the same time many— and certainly the authors of this report—think it necessary to find a way to proceed with research that promises to relieve some ills of the human condition. We focus on avoiding harms and maximizing benefits—that is to say, not on the rightness or wrongness of what we are doing, but on the results of what we are doing. Therefore, no red light.

That leaves the yellow, and we proceed with caution. We embed gene-editing research in regulatory controls. We suggest that research to which some or many object should not be undertaken "at this time." We focus on maximizing benefits and minimizing harms. All perfectly reasonable. But we do not ask ourselves whether there may be some research—even possibly beneficial research—that should not be done no matter what its benefits may be.

That is the nature of a yellow light. In theory it tells us to stop now; in practice it tells us to keep going—carefully. And whenever I see one, I always find myself thinking about what it means that we are proceeding with caution. On the one hand, we might congratulate ourselves. We are, after all, proceeding with caution, concerned lest we be misled by hubris. But on the other hand, it is still true that we are proceeding. We keep on going. We don't imagine that we should ever just stop. And so we keep on proceeding—doing so, moreover, with a good conscience, because we know that we are cautious, thoughtful, and morally concerned. It's just that, faced with the possibility of desirable consequences, we can never find a reason to stop.

No doubt it is generally wise to let a yellow light slow us down. But there may also be moments when we should remember that there always remains another possibility and that moral seriousness might sometimes be measured by our willingness to be as wise as kindergarteners and to know when to "stop, stop, stop."

BIBLIOGRAPHY

Banner, Michael. *The Ethics of Everyday Life: Moral Theology, Social Anthropology, and the Imagination of the Human*. Oxford: Oxford University Press, 2014.

National Academies of Science, Engineering, and Medicine. *Human Genome Editing: Science, Ethics, and Governance*. 2017. https://doi.org/10.17226/24623.

Ramsey, Paul. *Fabricated Man: The Ethics of Genetic Control*. New Haven: Yale University Press, 1970.

Sandel, Michael J. *The Case against Perfection: Ethics in the Age of Genetic Engineering*. Cambridge: Belknap Press of Harvard University Press, 2007.

III

Thinking Theologically:
Life's Ending

9

How Not to Write (or Think)
about Euthanasia[1]

A t its best Roman Catholic piety can be enormously powerful. It offers what we may call a way of affirmation—a sacramental understanding of the countless ways in which we meet the holy God in the everyday life of bodily gestures, repetitive prayer, candles, motherhood. And it does this without losing an equally powerful way of negation, which forbids us to suppose we can capture or control the presence of the transcendent God in such ways. But precisely because this intricate system of spiritual practice is so powerful, it can also go bad in powerful ways. Affirmation is safe only when negation is also present. One can become fascinated not so much with God as with one's own experience of candles, beads, genuflection, and a virgin mother. And then one may lose the transcendent otherness of that God in a way that would hardly be possible for, say, a serious Calvinism (which would, of course, have its own way of going bad).

This was, I have to confess, my first thought after reading "At His Own Wake, Celebrating Life and the Gift of Death," a *New York Times* (May 25, 2017) article about the death by euthanasia in Canada of a man named John Shields. Clearly intended to elicit pathos in its readers, the account is, by my lights, drowning in bathos. Let me admit straightforwardly at the

1. An earlier version of this essay appeared under the title "More Bathos than Pathos: How Not to Write about Euthanasia," *Commonweal* 144.13 (August 11, 2017).

outset: I don't much like the John Shields portrayed in this article, though he was much loved by some who knew him. I like even less some of the other characters who play significant roles in Mr. Shields's death—as, for example, Penny Allport, the "life-cycle celebrant" whose task it was to orchestrate and choreograph the homemade rituals, drawn from countless different (and incompatible) cultural and religious traditions, that shaped Mr. Shields's last hours and his death. I am not at all fond of Dr. Stefanie Green, who, needing "a better life-work balance" than her practice of maternity and newborn care permitted, turned to a focus on implementing Canada's year-old legalized "medical assistance in dying." "Birth and death, deliveries in and out—I find it very transferable," she says. "Both are really intense and really important." (Is it just an accident that the title of the *Times* article celebrates life—not the *gift* of life—while celebrating "the gift of death"? Perhaps the two are not so transferable after all.)

These are minor dislikes, however, compared with my reaction to the shameful inability of the *Times* and its journalist/reporter/essayist, Catherine Porter, to help readers not just to sympathize (as we should) with Mr. Shields in his suffering but also to think critically, distinguishing bathos from pathos. Evidently Ms. Porter was present as a silent participant throughout the events recounted in her article, an article the *Times* deemed important enough to run on its front page. Indeed, it is hard to detect any critical distance at all in her authorial voice. In the context of our society's deep divisions and confusions about the practice of euthanasia, this article amounts to a puff piece aimed at evoking support for one side of a complicated moral argument. A shorter piece on the op-ed page would have been more honest.

John Shields was evidently a man with great energy and a capacity to take interest in many aspects of life, though also in his own perceived "uniqueness." Ordained a priest in the Roman Catholic Church, he left after four years, though not before being prohibited from preaching and teaching at his parish in Austin, Texas. After that he became a social worker and, later, president of the British Columbia Government Employees' Union, over which he presided for fourteen years. After his first wife died of lymphoma he eventually married for a second time. He studied some Gestalt therapy, learned dowsing, and came to regard himself as a "spiritual cosmologist, believing that the universe was conscious and that everything was inextricably connected." Having left institutional religion for a kind of generalized spirituality strikes me as rather less countercultural than Mr.

Shields's self-image would suggest—and certainly far from unique. "I come forth at this precise moment to contribute my unique gifts to the great unfolding," he wrote in a memoir. And while this does not exactly bring Hegel to mind, we get the idea and can see why Ms. Allport would call his death his "great blooming."

His character was marked by the twists and turns of the several directions his life had taken. "He loved rituals, which began with the Catholic Masses of his childhood." To be of service was a central theme in his life, as was the theme of freedom. "He was always growing and exploring." Sadly, though, in his mid-seventies he was diagnosed with amyloidosis, a disease in which abnormal proteins accumulate in the body's organs, eventually causing death. Mr. Shields gradually lost feeling in and use of his arms and legs, finally having to enter hospice care. In his debilities he felt a loss of dignity, a diminished condition that he found "demeaning" and "unacceptable."

As it happened, the man and the moment were well matched. For only a year before Canada had legalized what it calls "medical assistance in dying." This permits not just assisted suicide but also euthanasia, in which a physician actually administers the death-dealing drugs. The law does prohibit euthanasia that is nonvoluntary—that is, when the dying person is, for whatever reason, no longer able to consent at the time the drugs are actually administered. This was in fact a worry for Shields and his wife: as his condition swiftly declined, they feared that, if he waited too long, he might be unable to give his consent when the chosen day arrived. And, in fact, it is hard to believe that this restriction can long survive—at least in British Columbia where, according to the *Times* article, an increasing number of patients are eagerly embracing euthanasia. Dr. Green herself, while adhering to the law's limits, suggests that there should be more "flexibility" in the law, a flexibility that would permit euthanasia for those who requested it before reaching a condition in which they are unable any longer to consent.

The Canadian law also specifies that, in order to qualify for euthanasia, an adult must be in an irremediable medical condition, experiencing suffering he or she finds intolerable, and likely to die fairly soon in any case. It is just as hard to believe that these conditions can hold for too long. Patients with severe but not life-threatening disabilities may well find their condition demeaning and undignified. Why exactly the fact that they are not likely to die soon should matter more than the felt indignity of their condition is far from clear.

In short, the Canadian law tries to ground permission for euthanasia in both compassion for those who suffer and a freedom to make important choices about the course and duration of one's life. But, as Daniel Callahan noted years ago, these criteria are on a collision course. If freedom and self-determination are this important—so important that we have a right to help in ending our life—how can we insist that such help may be offered only to those who are suffering irremediably? On the other hand, if the suffering of others makes so powerful a claim upon us that we should be willing to cause their death in order to end the suffering, it is not clear why we should limit our merciful help only to those who are still able to request it. After all, fully autonomous people are not the only ones who suffer greatly. We may suspect that the limits will gradually be extended.

Self-determination and compassion. Those are the two considerations upon which the case for euthanasia is based, and it is worth our thinking briefly about each. Living in a relatively individualistic society, it seems to us natural to say, "This is my life. Why shouldn't I be able to do with it as I please, so long of course as I hurt no one else in the process? I have been making important decisions along the path of life for years. Who should have the authority to tell me that I may not decide to end that life and to find a willing person to help?"

Understandable as this is, and appealing as it is bound to seem to almost all of us in certain moments, we need to remember that the basic premise is questionable. I may not do just anything I want with my life, for the rest of you will not permit it. The obvious case is that we do not permit others to sell themselves into slavery. But well short of that our freedom is restricted in other ways. We do not permit anyone to sell an organ for the best price offered. We penalize the sale or use of certain drugs. We prohibit polygamy.

Now, to be sure, about any of these we might wish to argue. Perhaps, as a way of addressing the shortage of organs for transplantation, we should permit the sale of a paired organ such as the kidney. Perhaps our society needs to adopt a more *laissez-faire* attitude toward the use of addictive drugs. Perhaps the time has come to reverse the prohibition of polygamy in our law. We can imagine reasoned public arguments about these—and other—constraints on our autonomy. But the point is that it then becomes a public argument, not a private assertion of autonomy. And we then need to offer each other reasons in support of our views. I may not simply say, "This is my life, and I may do with it whatever I want." Bumping up against the limits to my self-determination, I must realize that what we actually have here is a question about what it is reasonable (or not) to leave to private choice.

Perhaps, in fact, we can press just a bit more on the claim to self-determination. In class discussion years ago, one of my students, talking about a cousin of hers who had committed suicide and the effect that had on his family, said, "He didn't just take his own life; he took part of theirs as well." I went back to my office, wrote it down, and have been quoting her ever since, for that terrible experience had made her wise. She had come to see what is at least the beginning of wisdom: We are neither as independent nor as self-determining as we often imagine. It would be a shame not to have learned this before we come up against the fact of our mortality—a fact that inevitably mocks our pretensions to autonomy. We should not pretend to be self-determining as we near the end, claiming an illusory freedom to determine when the game is no longer worth the candle and asking others to sign on to that determination.

Compassion is at least as complicated as self-determination. If we really believe that we share an equal dignity with all other human beings, that belief ought to shape our understanding of compassion. It must be compassion for those who are our equals. Not a compassion of some who are gods for others who are human beings. Not a compassion of some who are human beings for others who are beasts lacking an equal dignity. Our equality is grounded in the fact that we do not make each other. Who does? Well, God does. Or, as John Shields would no doubt have preferred, Nature does. But we are equals because none of us can really claim to be a life-giver—someone who, on our own authority, may take the life of another human being or authorize another to take ours.

Thus, although compassion surely moves us to try to relieve suffering, there are things we ought not to do even for that worthy end—actions that would not honor or respect our shared human condition. One of the terrible truths that governs the shape of our lives is that sometimes there is suffering we are unable—within the limits of morality—entirely to relieve. Hence, the maxim that must govern and shape our compassion should be "maximize care," which may not always be quite the same as "minimize suffering." In our society, of course, the genuine Christian language of compassion has been greatly debased, and we will not learn how rightly to keep company with those who are suffering and dying unless we reclaim the limits that shape and govern it.

John Shields, alas, did not share such concerns. Of far greater significance, though, is the fact that the *Times* article, in its cloying way, never really raised them for serious exploration. So on the appointed day Mr. Shields, along with family and some friends, held his desired Irish wake before, not after, he died the next morning. I cannot bring myself to recount in detail the rituals devised by that life-cycle celebrant for Shields's "great blooming." The image of her crouching on the floor to thank the earth for carrying his body and summoning ancestors to guide his journey, which I will not soon forget, is like a *reductio ad absurdum* of the attempt to create one's own traditions and rituals. It is hard to believe that this sort of spirituality lite can for long sustain us in the face of death.

What are Christians to do in the midst of such cultural trends and their hagiographic celebration in the press? Perhaps we need to place a little less trust in our own spiritual insights and permit a genuinely transcendent, iconoclastic God to shatter our homemade pieties. We need to learn to live within the church's teachings and liturgies, allowing them to shape our feelings rather than supposing that our feelings should govern what we do. We need, in particular, to see to it that our funerals are less celebrations of our lives than testimonies to the hope of the resurrection and new creation. And in the face of a culture intent on teaching that to experience decline and loss of capacities is to lose dignity, we need to insist that each of us, whatever our capacities, is equidistant from eternity, and that no one for whom Christ was content to die can lack human dignity.

BIBLIOGRAPHY

Callahan, Daniel. *The Troubled Dream of Life: In Search of a Peaceful Death*. Washington, DC: Georgetown University Press, 2000.

10

Gifts of the Body

Procuring Organs for Transplant[1]

In many realms of life there are questions that never really go away. We
address them more or less satisfactorily, and for a time they recede from
the center of our attention. Yet, because they are important, they are likely
to reappear and again demand our consideration. In the realm of public
policy about bioethics one such question is whether it could be right to
increase the supply of organs for transplant by providing financial incentives for those who supply their organs, or even by establishing some kind
of market for the sale of organs. (Whether the market should work only for
sellers or for buyers also is, of course, one aspect of this recurring issue.)

Such questions have received attention in the past, but in recent years—
fueled by longer waiting lists for transplantation—they have returned to
the center of bioethical concern. In May 2006, the Institute of Medicine
(IOM) released a report (titled *Organ Donation: Opportunities for Action*)
that recommended against using financial incentives to boost organ supply.
The report did, however, propose some other means aimed at achieving the

1. An earlier version of this essay appeared in *The New Atlantis* 13 (Summer 2006).

same goal—in particular, increasing the rate of organ procurement from those who die suddenly of cardiac arrest. On May 15, 2006, responses to this report appeared on the op-ed pages of both the *New York Times* and the *Wall Street Journal*. Sally Satel (in the *Times*) and Richard Epstein (in the *Journal*) attacked the IOM report for its "timid," "narrow-minded," and "unimaginative" thinking. "The key lesson in all this," wrote Epstein, "is that we should look with deep suspicion on any blanket objection to market incentives—especially from high-minded moralists who have convinced themselves that their aesthetic sensibilities and instinctive revulsion should trump any humane efforts to save lives."

Although this is a serious challenge, it is, I think, a forgetful and a misleading one. Forgetful, because it has lost contact with the reasons that moved our society to turn to an organ procurement system based on giving (even if for a variety of motives, not all of which need be altruistic). Misleading, because in its animus against moralism it adopts a too simple moral position for which saving of lives always takes first moral priority.

The questions that need asking are not aesthetic but anthropological, and it would be a shame if we were to become tone deaf to such questions, however difficult to articulate they may be. So, for instance, we must ask: Even if we simply assume that there is a shortage of organs for transplant and that it is imperative that we overcome this shortage, how would we decide whether a market in organs was an acceptable way to meet that imperative? How decide without first asking ourselves what organs and bodies are? Or, how decide without asking ourselves who the person is who, with a kind of sovereign freedom, disposes—whether by gift or by sale—of bodily organs? After all, not everything is for sale, and we cannot decide whether a thing is a commodity that could properly be marketed without thinking about the kind of thing it is.

We are reluctant to think through such concerns, however, for we sense that they may raise disquieting questions about organ transplantation generally. So we are tempted to let them slide, and we prefer to begin in the midst of things, with particular questions that seem (even if deceptively so) more manageable. To his credit, Epstein sees this. In an earlier essay, he noted arguments Leon Kass had offered against the sale of human organs, arguments based in large part on the dignity of the embodied person, and then he put his finger on the point we prefer to avoid: "Taken at one level, Kass's arguments are so strong that they would preclude gifts as well as sales."

We have trained ourselves to think that organs are the sort of thing that can be given in the good cause of saving lives. But it now turns out that there are still more lives to be saved. Why then, exactly, are organs not the sort of thing that can also be sold in this same good cause? If we have learned to think of the organ as a separable part that can be offered to another, if we no longer see this offer as a kind of problematic self-mutilation, then it is hard to know why sale of these separable parts should be forbidden. The organs procured will save more lives and mitigate the shortage that operates as a given in the argument. What more need be said?

Perhaps, however, we should ask ourselves some very basic questions: In what sense is there a shortage of organs for transplant that *must* be overcome? On what basis, if any, should we suppose that the organs of one's body ought to be available for transplant into the body of another? Without making at least some progress in addressing these questions, I do not know how to think about whether proposals for increasing the number of organs for transplant—in particular, proposals for some sort of market in organs—make moral sense.

DEATH AS A PROBLEM TO BE SOLVED

If a man is dying of kidney failure, and if his life might be prolonged by a transplanted kidney but none is available for him, those connected to him by special bonds of love or loyalty may quite naturally and appropriately feel grief, frustration, even outrage. We are heirs of a tradition of thought that teaches us to honor each person's life as unique and irreplaceable (even though we may not be able really to make sense of this inherited belief apart from reference to the God-relation, which is uniquely individuating for each of us). Although the sympathy any of us feels is inevitably proportioned to the closeness of our bond with one who dies, we are right to honor the grief, frustration, and outrage of those who experience a loved one's death as tragic.

These quite natural feelings fuel the belief, widely shared in our society, that it is imperative to make more organs available for transplant; however, the same feelings of urgency and desperation also make it difficult to think critically about assumptions driving the transplant system in general. To take a very different example, we have on occasion experienced a "shortage" of gasoline in this country. Relative to the demand, the supply becomes scarcer than we would like. In the face of such a shortage, we could permit drilling in heretofore protected lands or we could ease the general demand for oil by developing alternative energy sources such as nuclear power. We could also learn to moderate our desires and demands for gasoline, altering the pattern of our lives. So there are ways to deal with the gasoline shortage that might work but would—at least in the eyes of some—exact too high a moral price. And there are ways to deal with the shortage that would teach us to modify our desires in such a way that we no longer think in terms of a shortage, but they would entail accepting certain limits on how we live. Upon reflection, we may well decide that neither of these answers to the gasoline shortage is a desirable direction to take, but it would be a frivolous person who continued to speak of a "shortage" without considering carefully both sorts of alternatives: exploring new sources of energy, or moderating our demands and expectations. Most of the time, though, when the subject is organ transplantation, we attend only to the search for new ways to procure organs. We look, as the subtitle of the IOM report puts it, for "opportunities for action."

If, however, we were to moderate the demands we make on medicine, we might be less pressured to think in terms of an organ shortage. Alongside our natural desperation at the impending death of one who cannot be replaced, alongside our natural tendency to see death as an evil to be combated, we must set another angle of vision about what it means to be human. Each of us is unique and irreplaceable; that is true. But each of us also shares in the limits of our finite condition; we are mortals. "The receiving of an organ does not," as William F. May once put it, "rescue the living from the need to die. It only defers the day when they will have to do their own dying." Tolstoy's Ivan Ilyich knew well the relentless logic of the syllogism: if all men are mortal, and if Caius is a man, then Caius is mortal. But that logic seemed both absurd and unjust when he tried to slot his own name, Ivan, into the syllogism in place of Caius.

We should not deny the existential anguish; we should also not deny the homely truth that each of our names can and will find its place in the syllogism. To refuse to acknowledge that second truth would turn medicine into nothing more than a crusade against death, plagued constantly by a "shortage" of cures for one or another deadly ailment. In other areas of medicine we are ready to brand that approach as inadequate, and recognition of our mortality ought to elicit similar caution when speaking about a shortage of organs for transplant. As Hans Jonas argued in one of the seminal articles of the bioethics movement in this country, progress in curing disease is not an unconditional or sacred commitment. The survival of society is not threatened when we do not conquer disease, however sad this may be for those who suffer.

From one angle, as long as one irreplaceable person dies whose life might have been prolonged through transplantation, there will always be an organ shortage. From another angle, that is just the truth of the human condition. If we turn organ procurement into a crusade, we make of death simply a problem to be solved rather than an event to be endured as best we can, with whatever resources of mind and spirit are available to us. To be sure, when a particular person—Ivan—faces death, we confront a problem that calls for our attention and our attempts to cure. But not only that. We also face the human condition that calls for wisdom and care. Sometimes, at least, we will undermine the needed wisdom and care if we think of this person's death as only or primarily a problem which it is imperative that we solve.

RECOVERING THE MEANING OF THE BODY

Freed of the sense that we are under some imperative to secure more organs, we may be able to think again of the price we would pay—perhaps, to be sure, a justified price—to increase the supply of organs for transplant. It may be that the limited supply of organs is due to thoughtlessness, selfishness, fear, or simply limited altruism. But it may also be based on weighty—if difficult to articulate—beliefs about the meaning of human bodily life. If our problem is thoughtlessness, selfishness, fear, or limited altruism, financial incentives might "solve" the problem. But if there are deeper reasons at work, reasons that have to do with what we may even call the sacredness of human life in the body, we pay a considerable price if we seize upon certain means to increase the supply of organs for transplant.

Perhaps, then, we should start with the disquieting possibility we might prefer to pass by. Forget the issue that arises further along the way, whether some kind of market in bodily organs could be morally acceptable. Start further back with the now widely shared presumption that it is morally acceptable—indeed, praiseworthy—freely to *give* an organ when this donation may be lifesaving. In the 1930 encyclical letter *Casti Connubii*, Pope Pius XI wrote, "Private individuals . . . are not free to destroy or mutilate their members, or in any other way render themselves unfit for their natural functions, except when no other provision can be made for the good of the whole body." How does one get from that to Pope John Paul II's words sixty-five years later in *Evangelium Vitae*? "There is an everyday heroism, made up of gestures of sharing, big or small, which build up an authentic culture of life. A particularly praiseworthy example of such gestures is the donation of organs, performed in an ethically acceptable manner, with a view to offering a chance of health and even of life itself to the sick who sometimes have no other hope."

John Paul's words notwithstanding, we would not ordinarily want a physician whose "treatment" harmed us in order to bring benefit to someone else. And ordinarily a surgeon would not think of operating on a person in order to help someone other than that person himself. For we know a person only in his or her embodied presence. In and through that body the person is a living whole. For certain purposes we may try to "reduce" the embodied person to a collection of parts, thinking of the person (from below) simply as the sum total of these parts. But we do not know, interact with, or love others understood in that way; on the contrary, we know them (from above) as a unity that is more than just the sum of their parts. The very idea of organ transplantation upsets these standard assumptions in a way that is problematic and that calls for justification.

PROCURING ORGANS FROM CADAVERS

Understandably, therefore, we are inclined to turn first to cadaver donation, to procuring organs for transplant from (newly) dead bodies. After all, it may not seem to raise these troubling questions so acutely. Even here, however, a certain caution is in order.

There is something uncanny about a corpse, for it is *someone's* mortal remains. We would, I think, worry about a medical student or a mortician who felt no need to stifle within himself a deep reluctance and contrary impulse the first time (or the hundredth time) he was called upon to handle or cut a human corpse. Reverence for the dead body is not (we think) entirely incompatible with using it for a good purpose, but surely there is much that this reverence would not permit. It is one thing—and not, we hope, incompatible with reverence—that medical students should, with fear and trembling, learn needed skills through dissecting a corpse. Would we think it equally unproblematic if corpses were dissected in high school biology classes? We accept that some people, out of a deep desire to serve the well-being of those who come after them, may give their corpses for dissection and study by medical students. Would we think it equally unproblematic if they freely donated their bodies for the manufacture of soap?

If we really freed ourselves of reservations and reverence, we could develop the "bioemporia" filled with "neomorts" that Willard Gaylin envisioned decades ago: repositories of brain-dead but breathing, oxygenating, and respiring bodies available for countless uses (medical training, drug testing, experimentation, harvesting of tissues and organs, and manufacturing). That few of us would be willing to turn in such a direction indicates, again, that certain deep human impulses must be overcome before we use the dead human body, even for the best of purposes—and not all uses would be acceptable to many of us, even were the body freely donated for such use.

That the corpse from which an organ is taken for transplantation is *someone's* mortal remains (and not just a collection of readily available organs) is also indicated by how hard it is for us not to think that the presence of a transplanted organ (or, at least, of certain organs) somehow brings with it the presence of the person from whom that organ was taken. Just such psychological complexities are at the heart of Richard Selzer's profound and provocative short story "Whither Thou Goest." When Hannah Owen writes to Mr. Pope seeking permission to listen for an hour to the heart of her deceased husband, which now beats in the body of Mr. Pope, she does so, as she puts it, because of "the predicament into which the 'miracle of modern science' has placed me." She professes no interest at all in Mr. Pope himself other than as one who houses something she used to know well and longs to hear again. Such is the mystery of the body and its parts, however, that a reader may wonder about this when, after finally receiving permission to listen to the heart now beating in Mr. Pope, Hannah is "nervous as a bride." For her, at any rate, the heart now beating in Mr. Pope's chest continues to carry the presence of her husband.

This is fiction, of course, but it may be profound humanistic wisdom as well. That the organ, the body, and the person for whom that body is the place of presence are not so easily separated in our psyches is well known. Thus, in *The Courage to Fail: A Social View of Organ Transplants and Dialysis* (first published in 1974), Renée Fox and Judith Swazey noted that "the gift of an organ may be unconsciously perceived by donor and recipient as an exchange through which something of the donor's self or personhood is transmitted along with his organ." Writing more than a decade later, in *Spare Parts: Organ Replacement in American Society*, Fox and Swazey had not found reason to change their mind. Many recipients of transplanted organs, they wrote, have "apprehension about absorbing a donated part of another known or unknown individual into his or her body, person, and life." Doing so evokes deeply buried "animistic feelings" people have about their bodily integrity, and they tend to feel that not just physical but also psychic qualities are transferred from the donor.

Thus, we should not too quickly assume that transplantation of organs even from a dead body is unproblematic. Those mortal remains retain the "look" of a person's life: not just a mechanism whose parts work together well or poorly, but the unity of that individual life. The mortal remains signify the history of that life in all its connections, especially with those to whom the person now dead was closely attached. It is not bad—indeed, it is highly desirable—that they should honor their shared history and mourn their loss by demonstrating reverence for that embodied life, and such reverence is quite a different thing from parceling out the component parts of a corpse for the sake of achieving desirable goals. In order to relieve suffering or save life some may overcome these considerable reasons for reluctance to give organs for transplant after death, but it would be deeply troubling if we experienced no reluctance that needed overcoming—if our thinking and acting were governed solely by the sense of an organ shortage that needed to be solved. "There is," as William F. May once put it, "a tinge of the inhuman in the humanitarianism of those who believe that the perception of social need easily overrides all other considerations."

CADAVERS (?) IN A LIMINAL STATE

Having come this far, we may also need to remind ourselves that the language of procuring "cadaver" organs for transplant is in some respects misleading. This is not the sort of cadaver upon which medical students hone their skills. Cadaver donation generally means taking organs for transplant from bodies which, though brain-dead and sustained entirely by medical technology, do not look dead. (Hearts still beat, blood still circulates, respiration continues.) The very concept of "brain death" that makes this liminal state possible has come under new challenge in recent years, and it is a challenge that needs to be faced, lest our criteria for death seem to be determined chiefly by our desire to procure organs for transplant.

It is striking, for example, that when organs are taken from a brain-dead but heart-beating corpse, the dead body is first anesthetized, lest its blood pressure rise precipitously. Thus, even the brain-dead body seems to manifest certain integrative functions. My point here is not to argue that we should return exclusively to cardiopulmonary criteria for determining death; on the contrary, there is still much to be said in favor of the concept of "whole brain death." Rather, I simply note that, even if this body with its heart still beating is a corpse, we would not bury it until it had "died all the way" (a formulation which, even if inexact, indicates that it is not foolish to think of such a body as in a kind of liminal state closely related to the condition of still living donors).

What we are in danger of losing here is a humane death. Indeed, death itself becomes a kind of technicality—an obstacle to organ procurement, which obstacle must be surmounted in order to procure the body's parts and accomplish our worthy purposes. This is especially evident in recent attempts, motivated again by a supposed imperative to diminish an organ shortage, to plan the deaths of patients in such a way as to procure organs almost immediately after the cessation of heart and lung activity. A patient on life support is prepared for surgery, taken to the operating room, given drugs that will protect the viability of his organs after death, removed from life support, declared dead two minutes after cardiac arrest—at which time his organs are removed for transplant. Thus, in an age that has worried greatly about having death occur in the dehumanizing context of machines and technology, our desperate sense that it is imperative to procure organs has led to precisely that: the loss of a humane death and acceptance of what Renée Fox called a "desolate, profanely 'high tech' death."

LIVING DONORS

We have yet to consider the truly living donor—not one in the liminal state of the brain-dead-but-heart-beating cadaver, but one who accepts injury to his or her body in order to relieve the suffering or preserve the life of another (usually, though not always, another to whom one is closely bound by ties of kinship or affection). Transplantation in these circumstances raises profound questions about the relation of organ(s), body, and person.

We need not question the charitable motives of the donor, even what Pope John Paul II termed the "heroism" of such an act. Nonetheless, it involves intending one's own bodily harm in order to do good for another. It is, as I noted earlier, the sort of thing a surgeon would normally not even consider doing. Indeed, near the dawn of the transplant age, noting the way in which our justifications of transplantation tend to imagine the person as "a spiritual overlord, too far above his physical life," Paul Ramsey suggested that, in the face of that exaltation of freedom to use the body for our purposes, physicians would "remain the only Hebrews," looking upon each person's life as a sacredness in the body. What, then, if anything, makes surgical mutilation acceptable—even good—in the context of transplantation?

One way to address this question would involve trying to overcome the close connection of organ, body, and person. We could train ourselves to think of the organ as entirely separable from the body, and the body as little more than a useful conveyance for the person. Thus, for example, Sally Satel suggested that thinking of the body's parts as not for sale is "outdated thinking." But partly because it is not easy so to train ourselves to think otherwise, and partly because the very difficulty of doing so suggests that there might be something dehumanizing about the attempt, we have turned in a quite different direction: the idea of donation. To think of the transplanted organ as a gift means that its connection to the donor's body remains and is recognized. Whatever psychological complications this may entail, it protects us against supposing that our bodies are simply collections of parts that could be "alienated" from ourselves in the way a thing or a commodity can be.

One who agrees to donate an organ gives himself or herself—not a thing that is owned, but one's very person. A gift—even a gift of something other than one's body—carries with it the self's presence in a way that a sale and purchase, for example, do not. This accounts, in fact, for the very strange mixture of freedom and obligation that is part of the experience of receiving a gift. One who gives has no obligation to do so and acts, therefore, with a freedom and spontaneity that are not possible for the one who receives that gift. And to receive it is to incur an obligation to use the gift with gratitude. If, to borrow an example from Paul Camenisch, I buy from a retiring professor a rare edition of Kant's works, I have not failed in any obligation of gratitude to him if a year later I give those works to a paper recycling drive. But if, having invested himself in those writings over the years, he now makes a gift of them to me, I am constrained to receive and use the gift with gratitude; for it carries his presence in a way that a purchased commodity could not.

It misses something, therefore, to say, as Robert Veatch does, that the donation model "is built on the premise that one's body, in some important sense, belongs to one's self." That model of ownership will sever the person from the body, and, once this has been done, it will be a short step to pretending (the psychology of it will be trickier) that the "donated" organ, being utterly alienable, retains no connection of any sort to the self who has given it. We have been wise not to think of our bodies that way, and, instead, to turn to the concept of donation as a way of conceptualizing for ourselves what happens in organ procurement and transplantation. To think otherwise would lose the human and moral significance of our bodies as the place of personal presence. The language of gift or donation is the only way we have, while permitting transplantation to go forward, to continue to honor the sense in which a person is an embodied whole, and the sense in which a transplanted organ carries with it continued attachment to the one who gives not just an organ but himself or herself.

We might, of course, even while continuing to think in terms of donation, try to make the gift seem less sacrificial. Especially when the organ is transplanted into a loved one with whom the donor's own well-being is bound up, it might make some sense to characterize it is as less a mutilation than a fulfillment (at some higher, spiritual level) of the self. Just as an organ might be surgically removed if that was necessary for the health of one's body, so also perhaps the good of the body might be subordinated to the well-being of the person as a whole. Roman Catholic moral theology has sometimes used a "principle of totality" to refer to this moral and spiritual wholeness of the person.

Certainly, however, such reasoning can take us only so far. If it may give a justifying rationale for donation of a kidney, we would probably draw back from similar reasoning used to justify the gift of a heart from a living donor. And the same thing would be true were we to forego this sort of reasoning (about a higher moral wholeness achieved by mutilation of one's body) and simply use the language of love and gift to explain the acceptability of harming one's own bodily self for the sake of another. Then, too, there would be limits to the kind of harm we would allow a living donor to incur: a kidney or even a portion of the liver, but not a heart.

But, one might ask, why? Why such limits to the "gift of life"? The only answer, I think, is that even when we override it for very important reasons, bodily integrity continues to be a great good that cannot simply be ignored in our deliberations. It continues to exert moral pressure, and, if it permits some gifts of the body, it does not permit any and all. And it exerts this pressure because the person (though more than just body) is present in and through the body—not as a mechanism composed of separable and readily alienable parts, but as a unified living whole that is more, much more, than simply the sum of those parts.

Unless we appreciate the deep-seated and legitimate reasons for hesitation about organ transplantation, we are likely to plunge ahead as if the weightiest imperative under which we labor were fashioning means to procure more organs. If, then, in order to try to solve a perceived shortage of organs, we turn to means of procurement that invite and encourage us to think of ourselves as spiritual overlords, free to use the body and its parts as we see fit in the service of good causes, we may save some lives, but we will begin to lose the meaning of the distinctively human lives we want to save. Even a practice of donating organs can be abused, of course. But permitting organ procurement only through the practice of donation allows us, even if just barely, to retain a sense of connection between the part and the whole, the person and the body—allows us, that is, not to destroy ourselves in seeking to do good.

BIBLIOGRAPHY

Camenisch, Paul. "Gift and Gratitude in Ethics." *The Journal of Religious Ethics* 9 (1981) 1–34.

Epstein, Richard A. "Organ Transplants: Is Relying on Altruism Costing Lives?" *The American Enterprise* 4 (1993) 50–57.

Fox, Renée C. "'An Ignoble Form of Cannibalism': Reflections on the Pittsburgh Protocol for Procuring Organs from Non-Heart-Beating Cadavers." *Kennedy Institute of Ethics Journal* 3 (1993) 231–39.

Fox, Renée C., and Judith P. Swazey. *The Courage to Fail: A Social View of Organ Transplants and Dialysis.* 2nd rev. ed. Chicago: University of Chicago Press, 1978.

———. *Spare Parts: Organ Replacement in American Society.* New York: Oxford University Press, 1992.

Gaylin, Willard. "Harvesting the Dead." *Harper's Magazine* 249 (1974) 163–70.

Jonas, Hans. "Philosophical Reflections on Experimenting with Human Subjects." In *Philosophical Essays: From Ancient Creed to Technological Man,* 105–31. Englewood Cliffs, NJ: Prentice-Hall, 1974.

May, William F. "Attitudes Toward the Newly Dead." In *Death Inside Out,* edited by Peter Steinfels and Robert M. Veatch, 139–49. New York: Harper & Row, 1974.

Ramsey, Paul. *The Patient as Person: Explorations in Medical Ethics.* New Haven: Yale University Press, 1970.

Veatch, Robert M. "Why Liberals Should Accept Financial Incentives for Organ Procurement." *Kennedy Institute of Ethics Journal* 13 (2003) 19–36.

11

Comforting When We Cannot Heal

The Ethics of Palliative Sedation[1]

I take as my starting point the following simple thesis: "Relief of suffering stands, next to health, as a crucial part of the medical goal, and medicine has always sought to comfort where it cannot heal." That sentence was first written by Leon Kass. I use it precisely because Kass is well known as a critic of expansive notions of the goals of medicine. He is disinclined to approve goals that stray too far from service to the good of health. And, of course, he has also written in opposition to the idea that physicians should (even from merciful motives) act with the purpose of ending a patient's life. Evidently he thinks those positions are quite compatible with the sentence I take as my thesis: "Relief of suffering stands, next to health, as a crucial part of the medical goal, and medicine has always sought to comfort where it cannot heal."

1. An earlier version of this essay appeared in *Theoretical Medicine and Bioethics* 39.3 (June 2018).

NO TO EUTHANASIA—YES TO DOUBLE EFFECT

Before turning more specifically to consider palliative sedation in light of this thesis, we need to stake out a position on more general questions that serve to frame anyone's thinking about this topic. We need, for one thing, to take a position on the matter of euthanasia. Is it permissible or not? After all, if there is no reason to draw back from the practice of euthanasia, there will be fewer cases in which we would need even to consider palliative sedation. Instead, we would simply proceed to end the suffering by dispatching the sufferer. The other question needing attention is the meaning and usefulness of "double effect" reasoning. If palliative sedation can reasonably be construed only as aiming at the patient's death, it will, in effect, be euthanasia—and, again, there will be little reason to draw back from frankly acknowledging that fact.

Obviously, we cannot here take up the matter of euthanasia with the thoroughness it deserves. We can, however, note all too briefly four considerations that are important to keep in mind when we ask ourselves whether euthanasia could be permissible.

First, a very simple point. Physicians are obligated to do what they can to relieve the suffering of their patients. But this means, what they "morally can." Physicians are not obligated to succeed. There can be no serious discussion of these matters if we do not acknowledge from the outset that there may be things physicians should not do even in order to relieve suffering. We cannot oppose medical hubris in other ways while ignoring it in these difficult circumstances. The physician is still a limited moral agent, and serious moral reflection always keeps open the possibility of limits on what may be done even in the best of causes.

Second, it cannot be emphasized too often that refusing to approve actions that intend (even for merciful motives) the death of a suffering person does not at all mean that we must do everything possible to keep that person alive. We should always choose life, not death, but the life we choose need not be the longest one available. Refusing or withdrawing life-prolonging treatment when it is either useless or excessively burdensome has been considered good medicine for centuries. One may rightly choose a life that is free of burdensome treatments even if also somewhat shorter than might be possible, so death need not always be opposed. Refusing to kill does not mean doing everything within our power to extend life. We should choose life, even if sometimes that means only how to live while dying.

Third, what about the freedom to order one's own life? We make countless decisions that shape the course our life takes. Why should others have the right to deprive us of the freedom to call a halt, if we think the time has come to do so? Powerful as such a question is within our culture, we need to remind ourselves that it is overstated by a good bit. There are many things—ranging from marrying one's sister, to using certain drugs, to selling a kidney for profit—that even our individualistic society will not allow any of us to do.

Moreover, we are never quite the independent individuals we like to suppose we are. In class discussion years ago one of my students, talking about a cousin of hers who had committed suicide and the effect it had on his family, said, "He didn't just take his own life; he took part of theirs as well." She articulated a deep sociological truth there, for our lives are connected to others from the start. At its deepest level, however, this truth is theological, not just sociological. Created by God for community with one another, created to know ourselves as finite beings for whom freedom becomes destructive if it acknowledges no limits, we deceive ourselves if we suppose that our lives are simply ours to do with as we please.

This also means—a fourth point we need to make—that genuine compassion for those who suffer must respect the boundary established by the fact that we are all equals, all equidistant from God. Our equality is grounded in the fact that we have not made each other. None of us is a life-giver. Hence, we cannot give ultimate authority over our life to another human being, nor are we authorized to exercise such authority over another. At least for Christians, therefore, compassion is not a formless emotion, free to be shaped in any way we please. Compassion does not move us to engineer another's death but to face it together. The most basic questions about the worth and meaning of human life are not for medicine to answer. All physicians can do—but it is a great deal—is to keep company with the dying when they confront, as each of us must, the question of the meaning and the point of the life we share.

This establishes a boundary—no to euthanasia—that should govern our thinking. If palliative sedation is just euthanasia by sleight of hand, then it will not be acceptable. If, however, it is relief of suffering grounded in the truth that we are not obligated to do everything within our power to prolong life, it may be permissible or even desirable. But in order to reflect upon what we are really doing when we practice palliative sedation, we need to take up a second preliminary question—the nature of double-effect moral reasoning.

At the heart of the concept of double effect is a distinction between what we *do* and what is *accomplished* by our doing. Much of the time we can reasonably foresee that any action we take is likely to have both good and evil results, both results we desire and results we would regret. Thus, I give a student a poor grade because that in fact is what his work merits, and he deserves an honest assessment of it. I may of course also hope that this will be a chastening experience, moving him to produce more diligent and careful work in the future, but whether this happens or not, he will have a truthful mirror in which to see clearly the quality of his work. Yet, knowing the student as I do, I may foresee that a poor grade is at least as likely to depress and dispirit him, making it even more difficult for him to produce good work, and contributing to a state of mind that may have long-term harmful effects on his life. Still, I am a teacher; he is my student; I owe him an honest assessment, and I owe fairness to other students whose work has been superior to his. So I intend to provide him with an accurate appraisal of his work, though I foresee the possible (perhaps likely) ill effects that may result. If I am morally culpable not only for what I do (what I aim at or intend) but also for all that I foresee resulting from what I do, then my hands are tied. I must give him a passing grade, perhaps even a pretty good passing grade, lest the foreseen evil effects come about.

That concept—of foreseen but unintended result—is the heart of double-effect reasoning, and we cannot get along without it. Without it a military leader cannot be justified in sending soldiers under his command out as a decoy. Without it a doctor cannot justifiably give a suffering patient increasing doses of a narcotic drug that may depress respiration and result in a somewhat hastened death. In fact, without the distinction between the aim and the result(s) of an action, anyone who threatens to do great evil if we ourselves refuse to do so can, in effect, hold us morally hostage, obligating us to do great evil.

This distinction between what we intend and what we foresee quite obviously is important for making moral judgments about how one ought to treat others. But it is just as important for judging one's own character. As responsible moral agents, we cannot think of our actions simply as impersonal events—done by someone who may be anyone. These actions both express and shape the persons we are. They are not simply events in the world; they are the occasions and opportunities in which we, so to speak, come upon ourselves, come to know who we are and of what we are capable. However good the cause, to aim at evil is not just to let that evil occur in the world. We cannot think of it simply as a byproduct of our attempt to accomplish some good. On the contrary, we have marked it with the personal involvement of our purpose. Put in Christian terms, this is to begin to make oneself a person who would not want to be with God.

To be sure, it is quite possible to play games with the language of double effect, but doing so will only foster skepticism about its worth. Thus, for example, imagine a soldier in combat who fires at an approaching enemy soldier and kills him. If we suppose that it is always wrong to aim to kill, but we want to defend the soldier's action, we might be tempted—as some have—to say that he aimed only to incapacitate the oncoming enemy, foreseeing but not intending his death. That, I fear, is the sort of argumentative move that makes skeptics of those who hear it.

Or, to take another example from warfare: Pilots might bomb a munitions supply depot, knowing full well that some civilians in the area are likely to be injured or killed. That is simply the sad reality of war and can be justified using double-effect reasoning. But if we know that a hospital and a school are fairly close to the munitions depot, and if nevertheless we make no effort to narrow our target as much as possible, nor ask our pilots to take risks in order to achieve that narrowing, we cannot reasonably claim that we intended to target only the munitions, foreseeing but not intending harm to those in the hospital or school.

Examples such as these make clear that what we aim at or intend is not just something inside us—what we want or desire, what moves us to act. On the contrary, the concept of intention must be distinguished from the concept of motive. Intention governs what we do, the structure of our action. And we cannot make an action mean just anything that we happen to want or desire.

Sometimes we may be uncertain how to make these distinctions, how to sort out the complications that thinking in terms of double effect requires of us. That is one reason why moral judgments may not always be easily transferrable to a court of law. But the fact that some of these cases are hard does not mean we should not draw the distinctions as best we can. Refusing to think in terms of double effect may seem to simplify matters, but it will be a simplicity that misses much of moral importance. All that can or should be asked of us is honesty, that we not play games with the language.

So then, yes to double-effect reasoning. It is both right and necessary to distinguish between our aim when acting and the results of that action.

Along with a no to euthanasia, that yes will also frame our consideration of palliative sedation.

THE "GOOD" OF CONSCIOUSNESS

Palliative sedation may be considered not only for patients who are in the very last stages of their dying but also for patients who (though suffering greatly) could live longer. For the moment, in order to keep things a little more manageable, I restrict my attention to patients whose physical and (related) emotional suffering is severe, whose pain has thus far not been effectively relieved, and whose death is imminent—a matter of hours or days. A physician might approach caring for such a patient in two ways that seem rather similar but may not be.

On the one hand, a physician could gradually increase dosages of pain medications, hoping to find a point at which the patient can tolerate his pain, while of course foreseeing that the increasing dosages might decrease the patient's level of consciousness and might shorten life somewhat by suppressing respiration. This is, almost classically, an instance of double-effect reasoning—aiming at the good effect of relieving distressing symptoms, while foreseeing and allowing the evil effects of possibly shortened life and diminished consciousness. And something like this, I assume, is what clinicians opposed to palliative sedation would do in caring for their patients.

On the other hand, a physician could use a barbiturate drip intended to render the patient unconscious, thereby eliminating the patient's experience of suffering during the last hours or days of life. This approach differs from the first in that this second physician takes aim not at physical symptoms that are producing pain and suffering, but at the conscious experience of suffering itself. We might also try to use the language of double effect here, saying for example: The physician's action aims at the good effect of rendering the patient unconscious and, hence, free of experienced suffering, while foreseeing and allowing the evil effect of a possibly shortened life.

But that formulation forces us to think about a significant difference between the two possible approaches I have sketched. May we properly describe unconsciousness as a good for this patient—or for any human being? May we properly describe an intention to render a patient unconscious as, in these difficult circumstances, good medical practice? Or must we say that the second physician aims at an evil effect—namely, unconsciousness—as a means to achieving the good effect of relieving suffering? The language of double effect can work for the second approach only if, sometimes, unconsciousness is not an evil but a good at which it is permissible to aim—and that, in fact, is the position I want to defend.

We can, of course, understand why one might hold that it is always wrong for a physician deliberately to induce unconsciousness in a patient. Physicians, we might say, serve the good of health, and consciousness is an important aspect of what we mean by health. Hence, although physicians may sometimes render a patient temporarily unconscious (say, while performing surgery), that is always part of a procedure whose overall goal is bettering or restoring the patient's health. In no way does it express an intention to turn against the good of consciousness, an intention that (on this view) should have no place in good medical practice.

This is a serious argument, but I myself do not find it persuasive. Granting, of course, that different patients may value differently continuing conscious experience, consciousness seems to me, if I may put it a little too brashly, not quite that big a deal. Imagine, for example, that you have for years been an insulin-dependent diabetic and are now irretrievably dying from an incurable cancer, only days from death. May you, having said your prayers and your goodbyes, stop taking insulin and drift off into a diabetic coma? Or are you obligated to remain conscious for those last days while suffering the effects of your cancer? I cannot see that there is any obligation to continue the insulin, any obligation to remain conscious, in such circumstances. In doing without the insulin, such a person would not be choosing death; he would simply be choosing how to live while dying.

I was not conscious at the start of my life in the womb, was barely conscious after birth, and (wholly apart from anything doctors do) may not be conscious at life's end. That is to say, life has a trajectory of development that takes us from rudimentary beginnings, to what we like to think of as optimal capacities, to diminished capacities, to loss of many or most capacities (including perhaps consciousness) at the end. To the degree that consciousness is a good, it is so only in terms of that pattern of development. As I would not ordinarily try to suppress consciousness in a healthy thirty-five-year-old, so I would not ordinarily be bothered by its absence in a fetus or feel any need to foster or extend its expression in a ninety-five-year-old who has said his prayers and his goodbyes. That is to say, I think about consciousness rather in the way I think about our procreative powers. Each is a part of good health, a part of the good physicians serve, but each has a limited place in the overall trajectory of a life.

Physicians serve the good of health, to be sure. But not only health. Relief of suffering is also one of the goals of medicine, and physicians must seek to comfort even when they cannot heal. By hypothesis we are considering a patient whose death is imminent, whose suffering is terrible, and for whom even considerable doses of medication to relieve pain symptoms have been unsuccessful. Remembering that one of the goals of medicine is relief of suffering, I believe that sedation to unconsciousness for such a patient, even if rarely needed, can be good medical practice. In such straitened circumstances there is no need for, and little to be gained from, attempting to distinguish an intention to palliate symptoms (with the foreseen effect of unconsciousness) from an intention to produce unconsciousness. Just as we strain double-effect reasoning beyond its limits if we think of the soldier who fires at an enemy as aiming only to incapacitate rather than to kill, so also here we should simply acknowledge that in rare circumstances we rightly intend to produce unconsciousness in the patient.

No doubt, as I have said, such cases will be relatively rare. But, subject of course to correction by those with medical training and experience, I think there are such cases. Here is one. It seems to me indubitable.

In his book *Dying Well*, Ira Byock, certainly a well-known hospice physician and a critic of proposals for euthanasia, tells the story of a woman named Terry Matthews. She was suffering terribly from an advanced kidney cancer, was in the end being given dosages of 900 milligrams of morphine per hour—yet remained in unconquerable pain, as she struggled to remain alive for her husband and children. Finally, when she could bear it no longer, Dr. Byock gave her a barbiturate drip that would, as he writes, "put her into a deep, painless sleep," in which sleep she could die peacefully. Recounting the case, he says that he told her, "I can give you a sedative . . . that will make you drowsy and then put you into what we call a 'twilight sleep.'" She asks whether she will still wake up sometimes and find herself again in this terrible pain. "No, Terry," he replies, "not if you don't want to." Having expressed to the end her love for her husband and children, she then accepted sedation and died a little more than a day later, never having regained consciousness.

I cannot describe this as bad medical practice, and, hence, it seems to me to be a case in which intending to sedate to unconsciousness is good and morally appropriate medical care. Perhaps—I cannot say—some other patient could have tolerated the pain Terry Matthews endured, though (given Byock's description) I find that hard to believe. We need only one such case to remind us that "relief of suffering stands, next to health, as a crucial part of the medical goal, and medicine has always sought to comfort where it cannot heal." I conclude, therefore, that it cannot always be morally wrong to turn against the good of consciousness.

HARDER CASES

Not always. But the previous discussion was confined very specifically to instances of patients whose physical and (related) emotional suffering is severe, whose suffering has thus far not been effectively relieved, and whose death is imminent—a matter of hours or days. There are certainly harder cases—for example, of those who despite suffering terribly may yet live for some time, or those whose suffering is for the most part emotional rather than physical (that is, whose suffering is "existential"). Such cases need more particular attention. In taking them up I will say once more here, and will not repeat continually, that I am not a physician. My understanding of cases is therefore always subject to refinement or correction by those with more exact knowledge. At any rate, consider a series of three possible cases.

Suppose a seventy-five-year-old man, who underwent surgery for colon cancer five years ago, and has now entered the hospital with symptoms of severe abdominal pain and vomiting. Tests show that his bowel is obstructed and that his cancer has returned and spread into both abdomen and bones. He has at most perhaps a month or two to live, and his physicians treat him with high doses of narcotic drugs to ease his pain. Unfortunately, the side effects of those drugs, constant muscle twitching and nausea, are almost impossible for him to tolerate. After a week of this treatment in the hospital, and with the bowel obstruction exacerbated rather than resolved, he finds himself at the end of his tether and asks to be sedated until he dies. Since, in his case, it would make little sense to pump nutrients into his body, he would not be given artificial nutrition and hydration if sedated to unconsciousness. Very likely, then, he may die somewhat sooner than if he were not sedated, although, of course, since severe pain can also shorten life, we cannot be certain.

This is a harder case than that of Terry Matthews. It may be less clear that this man's pain is intolerable, though it is certainly very bad, and his death, though not that far off, is not quite imminent. Still, even if not every person in his condition would make the request he does, I do not think he does wrong in asking to be sedated; it is permissible for him to choose to live this way—unconsciously—while dying. Nor do I think his physicians do wrong if they comply with his request.

But it is important to be clear about why one might say this. In its 2014 position statement on palliative sedation the Board of Directors of the American Academy of Hospice and Palliative Medicine defended the use in "extreme situations" of sedation to unconsciousness, but only if "its use is not expected to shorten the patient's time to death." In my view, that formulation is unsatisfactory. In the case I have described here, "the patient's time to death" could possibly be shortened somewhat if he were continuously sedated. But that would be, in the language of double effect, a foreseen but unintended effect of an action properly aimed (or so it seems to me) at relieving suffering that the patient was unable to tolerate despite the best of care short of sedation. He is going to die soon in any case, and I cannot see that physicians are obligated to see to it that he remains conscious until the very end. Assuming they have done their best—and failed—to provide tolerable relief of his symptoms by means short of sedation, I think they could rightly comply with his request.

Imagine next a patient with relatively advanced ALS—still able to breathe without constant support of a ventilator, but no longer able to stand, to walk, or to use his arms and hands effectively. He remains able to chew food and eat but has on a number of occasions choked while eating, an experience that is, of course, terrifying. Clearly at some future time, whose nearness is difficult to predict, his disease will progress to the point where, without permanent respiratory support, he will be unable to breathe and will die. But that is still sometime in the indefinite future. He is, however, terrified by what the future holds and asks to be sedated until he dies.

Notice that although this patient's debilitating physical condition is the source of much of his suffering, those physical symptoms in themselves are not the reason he requests sedation. He is asking for relief from feelings of fear, terror, and (perhaps) a sense of recoil from his physical inabilities and dependence. Complicating his case, however, is that he may still have some time to live. If we sedate him to unconsciousness and do not provide him with nutrition and hydration, he will almost surely die sooner than he would otherwise. Doing that begins to look more like choosing death than simply choosing how to live while dying. Of course, if we were to sedate him and simultaneously tube feed him, that would be a different matter, for then relief of suffering, not death, would clearly be our aim.

Hence, the patient must ask himself what it is that he in fact intends, and what it is that he wants the physician to help him do. Is he choosing death, aiming at it as his desired end? Or is he simply choosing one from among the several possible life choices still available to him? And physicians must ask themselves what they are doing; for sedating him while providing nutrition is doing something different from sedating him while providing no nourishment. Physicians will have to judge what constitutes good medical practice in such circumstances. Understandable as this patient's request is—after all, in similar circumstances I would be just as terrified—it is hard to think of sedation without nutrition in this instance as a choice of life, not death, and we should think twice before distorting double-effect language to make it seem otherwise. Rather than turning to sedation in such a case, perhaps physicians should seek for the patient forms of spiritual and psychological care that can directly address the fear and desperation he is experiencing—and in that way keep company with him in the midst of his suffering. To be sure, such care may or may not help the patient deal with his fears, but, as I noted earlier, physicians (and other caregivers) are not obligated to succeed.

Permanent sedation is even more problematic for patients whose suffering is, so far as we can tell, a result not of an underlying physical pathology but a product of beliefs they hold about their life. For example, they may think their life no longer has purpose or meaning, they may experience a deep sense of worthlessness or disgust with themselves, or they may be deeply distressed by the loneliness and dependence of old age. It should not be impossible for us to understand and sympathize with them. But they are not dying and, hence, cannot choose how to live while dying. In truth, life is precisely what they do not want to choose.

Granting that there is no easy recipe for dealing with such deep-seated existential distress, at the heart of our humanity is an affirmation of life—a sense that our psychic and spiritual well-being requires that, with the help of others, we face our own fragility, seeking personal and spiritual wholeness. Turning to sedation in such cases seems more like abandoning patients than keeping company with them. It would be hard to claim with a straight face that the shortened life of such patients is simply a foreseen and not also an intended consequence of sedation to unconsciousness.

There is, of course, no end to such cases. But by thinking about these few examples, I hope at least to have refined and sharpened somewhat our approach to them. I take what I have done as attempting to illustrate what physicians have always known—that they should never aim to kill, but that relief of suffering stands alongside restoration of health as central to the goals of medicine, and that physicians must try to comfort where they cannot heal. The vocation of the doctor is, as Paul Ramsey once put it, to adhere to the old medieval aphorism "to cure sometimes, to relieve often, and to comfort always"

BIBLIOGRAPHY

Byock, Ira. *Dying Well: Peace and Possibilities at the End of Life.* New York: Riverhead, 1997.

Kass, Leon R. *Toward a More Natural Science: Biology and Human Affairs.* New York: Free Press, 1985.

Ramsey Paul. *The Patient as Person: Explorations in Medical Ethics.* New Haven: Yale University Press, 1970.

12

Christian Living toward Dying[1]

"**A** theology whose central message is the biography of a crucified Jew cannot avoid speaking about death, whether it be his death or ours." True as those words of Jaroslav Pelikan are, there is probably no single best way to speak of death. Here, though, I will take my direction from Karl Barth's repeated attempts to think about our humanity from three different—though complementary rather than competing—angles of vision, which correspond to God's action in creation, reconciliation, and redemption. These three angles invite us to think about death as an aspect of created life, as judgment on our disordered lives, and as a power that will one day be overcome in the new creation God promises. Indeed, Christian moral reflection on almost any important topic—in this case, the death toward which we move—cannot bypass any of these three angles of vision.

Of course, even those who do not begin from within the contours of this Christian story may still come to understand some truth about human nature, but they are less likely to see the truth about human destiny. For if our vision is restricted to created life but does not include reconciled and redeemed life, we will have little to say about the life God promises in the new creation. At best we will think in terms of something rather like an

---

1. An earlier version of this essay appeared under the title "Resting in the Peace of Jesus: Christian Living toward Dying," in *Christian Dying: Witnesses from the Tradition*, edited by George Kalantzis and Matthew Levering (Eugene, OR: Cascade, 2018).

indefinitely extended continuation of this life, and sooner or later it will become clear that we cannot make sense of such a notion.

Thus, for example, the philosopher Samuel Scheffler suggests that, understandable as it may be that we might "wish that our lives could go on forever," that wish is "confused." Rather than enhancing the pleasure we take in life, living forever would, Scheffler thinks, actually undermine the kind of value life has. For that value depends on the limitations of natural, finite life. "A life without temporal boundaries would no more be a life than a circle without a circumference would be a circle. So whatever the eternal existence of a being might be like, it would not be just like our lives only more so." Scheffler can make little sense of imagining creatures who are like us but who do not experience the kinds of bodily limits that characterize our experience. Such creatures would never have to act or make decisions "against the background of the limits imposed by the ultimate scarce resource, time. But every human decision is made against that background, and so in imagining immortality we are imagining an existence in which there are, effectively, no human decisions."

Scheffler is a distinguished philosopher, and we have little reason to disagree with him on his own terms. But we need not confine ourselves to those terms. Because we love, trust, and hope in Jesus—who was not simply resuscitated on the third day but (rather) raised to a life that is genuinely new and not just more of the same—our understanding of death can and must be shaped by a more expansive vision. That, at any rate, is my aim here—to think of death within the entire history of redemption. To that end I will make use of three stanzas from a hymn by the nineteenth-century Norwegian pastor Magnus Landstad: "I Know of a Sleep in Jesus' Name."

CREATED LIFE

> I know of a peaceful eventide;
> And when I am faint and weary,
> At times with the journey sorely tried,
> Thro' hours that are long and dreary,
> Then often I yearn to lay me down
> And sink into blissful slumber.

Our days and years are lived out east of Eden, and it is for our good that the cherubim with flaming sword stand guard, lest any of us should seek a way to the tree of life. This earthly life could never satisfy the deepest desire of the human heart, and, hence, it is good that the course of life should move through decline to death. That is the truth about created human life, but we can begin nearer to the ground.

Created life is a gift, but also a burden. We are living organisms, bodies animated by soul. That is, we are not just "things," not inanimate objects. This is especially clear in the German language, which makes a distinction not present in many other languages—the distinction between *Leib* and *Körper*. Lacking soul, our bodies are purely material things, corpses. To be living organisms is, therefore, a great gift; yet, as Hans Jonas noted in a profound essay on mortality as both burden and blessing, it is a gift that comes to us also as a task. We call that task metabolism. Through constant exchange of substances with our environment we sustain our existence as living beings. This means, however, that we constantly hover "between being and non-being." We cannot just persist indefinitely, the way a rock is "simply and fixedly what it is, identical with itself over time, and with no need to maintain that identity by anything it does."

For us, by contrast, continuing to live is always a task, sometimes a burdensome task, and we have life "strictly on loan." Because we are finite organisms, the course of human life, unless ended prematurely by illness or accident, has a natural trajectory of growth and development through decline to death. Sooner or later the fires of metabolism burn themselves out, and *Leib* becomes *Körper*. And thus, as the poet John Hall Wheelock writes, "The dead are the only ones who never die."

Our time is never unlimited; it is always what Karl Barth called an "allotted time." That does not make it any less a gift. It simply means that our time is not God's timeless eternity, and it invites us constantly to remember that we are not Creator but creatures. It seems right, therefore, that Odysseus, offered the choice between an immortal life with the nymph Calypso and a return home to his wife, Penelope, should choose the latter. He chooses, that is, to be a man, not a god, accepting a life that is strictly on loan and that moves inevitably toward death. For that is the nature of our allotted time, a time in which decline must come and, sooner or later, we grow "faint and weary."

To acknowledge that it is a burden to maintain our life over time does not mean that this life lacks goodness or sweetness. Quite the contrary. This is a world that invites our love. "Shall not a man sing as the night comes on?" Wheelock asks. Although we know that sooner or later the fires of metabolism burn themselves out in our bodies, "[t]he fury and joy of every sound and sight" along the way cannot and should not be denied. It is right that we should love these sounds and sights, right that we should enjoy the beauty of life, right even that we should say, as the poet does, "More time— oh, but a little more." Desire for longer life and grief at the death of those we love are not wrong for Christians. Our funerals are not—or should not be—simply celebrations of life and rejoicing that the deceased loved one is now "in a better place." They should be occasions for sadness, even if we acknowledge that the one we loved has arrived at a "peaceful eventide" and a "blissful slumber."

About finite human life we must always, therefore, say both that its sweetness elicits our love and that, in the end, it will fail us. Describing St. Augustine in his classic study of the *City of God*, J. N. Figgis captured this two-sidedness in its most pronounced form.

> In Augustine there were struggling two men, like Esau and Jacob in the womb of Rebecca. There was Augustine of Thagaste, of Madaura, of Carthage, of Rome, of Milan, the brilliant boy, the splendid and expansive youthful leader, "skilled in all the wisdom of the Egyptians," possessed of the antique culture, rhetorical, dialectic, Roman—the man of the world, the developed humanist with enough tincture of Platonism to gild the humanism; and there is the Augustine of the "Confessions," of the "Sermons," of the "De Civitate," the monk, the ascetic, the other-worldly preacher, the biblical expositor, the mortified priest. These two beings struggle for ever within him, the natural man filled with the sense of beauty and the joy of living, expansive, passionate, artful—and the supernatural Christian fleeing from the world, shunning it, burning what he adored, and adoring what he burnt, celibate and (at times) almost anti-social.

Surely it is understandable that we should desire more of this life and that only with difficulty can we learn to accept that our bodies must wither and decline.

But the deepest truth remains that of the angel with the flaming brand at Eden: More of this life could never fully satisfy our love's longing, for what we want is not simply quantitatively more of this life, but a beauty that is qualitatively different. "In other words," Josef Pieper writes, "the allaying of the thirst cannot consist simply in the mere continued existence of the thirster." We know ourselves as people who are always on the way, always wanting a fulfillment not yet given.

Thus, both aspects of our creatureliness—the limits of our finite condition, and the inner freedom to soar beyond those limits in longing for a good not yet fully possessed—suggest that, however lovely this life may be, death cannot simply be bad for us. On the one hand, the limits of our finitude help to shape and form lives that are distinctively human. To be finite organisms, animated bodies, is to live a life that has not just duration but also a characteristic shape—from infancy, through maturity, to decline and death. The moments of such a life are not identical; they take their specific character from their place in the whole. That is what a distinctively human—and limited—life is like. And on the other hand, the metabolic exchanges by which we work to sustain ourselves as animated bodies also bear witness that a human being cannot be reduced to the matter of those exchanges, for they indicate, as Jonas observes, that a human being has "a sort of freedom with respect to its own substance, an independence from that same matter of which it nonetheless wholly consists." This life has its own special beauty, but it does not finally quench the thirst it evokes in us. As a character in Wallace Stegner's novel *The Spectator Bird* says, "A reasonably endowed, reasonably well-intentioned man can walk through the world's great kitchen from end to end and arrive at the back door hungry."

Eventually, therefore, we need to come "faint and weary" to "eventide," yearning to "sink into blissful slumber." That is the truth of our created life.

RECONCILED LIFE

> O Jesus, draw near my dying bed
> And take me into Thy keeping
> And say when my spirit hence is fled,
> "This child is not dead, but sleeping."
> And leave me not, Savior, till I rise
> To praise Thee in life eternal.

Thus far, limiting our perspective to created life, we have noted two reasons for thinking that death is not necessarily bad for human beings. Because we are created as living bodies, death is built into the shape of a meaningful human life. And because we are created with a thirst for God, more of this same life could never answer to the love that moves us. How is it, then, that St. Paul characterizes death not as a good to be desired but as the wages of sin and the last enemy? Evidently death is not only the natural end of human life but also something other and more than its natural end.

To a limited extent we can make sense of this on the basis of ordinary human experience. If created life is filled with beauty and sweetness, then its loss is reason for sadness. If we seem to be characterized by a thirst never satisfied in this life, death might seem to announce that our created life is vain and futile. But sadness and futility do not quite add up to judgment or punishment, and the fact that death comes to every living organism cannot fully reconcile us to it. For *my* death is not merely a participation in what is universal, what is common to all human beings. My death is also unique. That is the point of Ivan Ilyich's often quoted reflections on the standard syllogism: "All men are mortal, Caius is a man, therefore Caius is mortal." This, Ilyich reflects, "had always seemed to him correct as applied to Caius, but by no means to himself. That man Caius represented man in the abstract, and so the reasoning was perfectly sound; but he was not Caius, not an abstract man." On the contrary, he had been a little boy with a particular mother and father, particular toys, particular school experiences, particular loves. "Caius really was mortal, and it was only right that he should die, but for him, . . . Ivan Ilyich, with all his thoughts and feelings, it was something else again. And it simply was not possible that he should have to die. That would be too terrible."

However true it may be, therefore, to note that our finite life must inevitably move toward its end, Pelikan reminds us that death "as it actually encounters us" has the character of judgment, for it encounters us "as sinful and guilty men." We may say that one who dies has "passed" or "passed away," but those comfortingly benign formulations fail to articulate the real truth. For one who dies has been summoned—summoned for judgment. Pelikan notes that Cyprian—bishop of Carthage in the mid-third century AD—seems to have been the first Latin writer to use the word *arcessitio* ("summons") to refer to death. That summons is no gentle "passing" from this life, perhaps to a better place. "To Cyprian the idea of the summons connotes the authority of the Supreme Judge to order a man into his presence and to demand an account from him of all that he has been and done." To simply "pass away" in death may be sad, but it does not really call us into question. If, however, death is a summons, then it confronts us with "the irresistible call of the Summoner"—to personal encounter with One who rightly judges us. If ever we had thought we were in charge of our own lives, we now will see how vain such notions were.

As Ivan Ilyich understood, the summons is in no way abstract; it is directed to each of us individually, and it judges our loves as misdirected. So the Letter to the Hebrews notes, "It is appointed for men to die once, and after that comes judgment." How is it that, in the face of such judgment upon our misdirected loves, we might nonetheless find the faith to say "come, sweet death" to such a summons?

That happens only as we pray, "O Jesus, draw near my dying bed / And take me into thy keeping." For, as the Letter to the Hebrews also notes, if we must die once and face judgment, so also "Christ, having been offered once to bear the sins of many, will appear a second time, not to deal with sin but to save those who are eagerly waiting for him." When we rest in the peace of Jesus, faith trusts what is not necessarily evident to sight. Jesus freely submits to death as *judgment*, not simply as biological necessity. As the "first-born among many brethren," he takes upon himself the judgment of all, "to put away sin by the sacrifice of himself." He is, therefore, as Karl Barth so aptly put it in volume IV/1 of his *Church Dogmatics*, "the judge judged in our place."

Here faith discerns the answer to Ilyich's bewilderment at the particularity of his death, a death that he cannot and should not experience as generic. If each of us dies as a unique individual, each of us is also uniquely one for whom Jesus is the judge judged in our place. Meditating upon his own brush with death, Richard Neuhaus once recalled Potter's Field on Hart Island in New York City. There thousands of unclaimed dead, once particular lives now reduced to nameless corpses, have for almost two centuries been buried in numbered boxes. But in the middle of Potter's Field a large stone stands, inscribed with the words, "He Knows Them by Name." Each may be but a number in Potter's Field, but before God none is merely a generic human being.

This truth, that God knows each of us by name, has particular significance in the case of those who die—as we say from the perspective of our finitude—"prematurely." They do not enjoy a full life with its characteristic shape from infancy, through maturity, to decline and death. And if the meaning and worth of life were judged only from the perspective of the shape of a full life, and not also by remembering that in every moment of life we are equidistant from God, premature death of one whom we love might well lead us to despair. But the days or weeks of a child who dies soon after (or even before) birth are not only days of a life tragically cut short, though of course they are that from the perspective of a normal lifespan.

They are also the days or weeks of a God-aimed spirit, whose every moment is lived before One for whom a thousand years are but as yesterday when it is past, and they do not count less or have any less worth because they never progress to maturity or old age. Jesus will draw near such a child's dying bed as surely as he will the deaths of those who live out their allotted threescore years and ten—or, if by reason of strength, still more.

In the end, then, the One who summons each of us at death is One with the power and authority to say, "This child is not dead, but sleeping." To be sure, it is, in the words of the Letter to the Hebrews, "a fearful thing to fall into the hands of the living God." But, as Barth says, when that living God is the judge judged in our place, we "fall into *His* hands and not the hands of another."

REDEEMED LIFE

> I know of a morning bright and fair
> When tidings of joy shall wake us,
> When songs from on high shall fill the air
> And God to His glory take us,
> When Jesus shall bid us rise from sleep—
> How joyous that hour of waking!

Misdirected as our loves often are, faith trusts that they can be redeemed—and so, we live in hope for life beyond death. We should not too quickly suppose, however, that there is nothing at all analogous to death in the promised life to come, nor should we suppose that entry into God's own eternal life must entirely await the end of this life.

May we not say, subject of course to the proviso that for now we speak from faith not sight, that in the life of the triune God there is, as C. S. Lewis puts it, something akin to dying—a kind of "continual self-abandonment"? From eternity the Father gives all that he is and has to the Son, who offers that begotten life back to the Father in perfect obedience, through the bond of love that is their Spirit. Entirely at one in their self-giving, each of the three persons is characterized, as Lewis suggests, by self-abandonment, each losing itself in their shared work that is marked by neither jealousy nor strife. When the Son offers himself on the cross in human history, he does here among us what he does from eternity in the glory of his Father. Hence, Lewis, picturing the eternal life of the triune God as a dance in which each continually abdicates his place and gives way to the other, writes, "All pains and pleasures we have known on earth are early initiations in the movements of that dance," though Lewis adds (no doubt calling St. Paul to mind), "but the dance itself is strictly incomparable with the sufferings of this present time."

It is also true that the promised life of the new creation touches us even now, as we still live toward death. "If anyone is in Christ, he is [present tense!] a new creation," St. Paul writes in 2 Corinthians, enunciating in his own idiom the Johannine teaching that to know Jesus, whom the Father has sent, is life eternal. To be baptized into Christ is to begin a pilgrimage toward the full realization of a redeemed life in which we already share. Thus, in his *Small Catechism* Luther describes baptism as signifying "that the old Adam in us with all sins and evil desires is to be drowned and die through daily contrition and repentance, and on the other hand that daily a new person is to come forth and rise up to live before God in righteousness and purity forever." This means that the death toward which we live is the last gasp of a life the Holy Spirit has been putting to death in us since our baptism, and the redeemed life we will share in the new creation is the full realization of "the first fruits of the Spirit," already present in our life here and now.

Of course, acutely aware as we are of the truth St. Paul enunciates— that "our outer nature is wasting away" day by day and that we have not yet put on the promised "eternal weight of glory"—we can only live in hope. Which means, inevitably, that we must ask, For what exactly do we hope? And this is by no means an easy question to answer. We hope to rest in the peace of Jesus, to be taken into the imperishable, eternal life of God. That promised eternal life is not simply an immortal, bodiless life—for, after all, as Pelikan notes, the existence of the fallen angels should remind us that in itself "there is nothing desirable about living forever."

Nor is the promised life easily thought of simply in terms of a continued existence of the soul apart from the body. To be sure, there is something quite natural about that way of thinking. Contrasting an inner and outer self captures something true to our lived experience. As truly as I know that the component parts of my body are constantly being replaced throughout life, I also have a sense that in, with, and under this constant change I—what we are pleased to call my "self"—somehow persist. Nevertheless, if a human person is the *union* of soul and body, if that is what a genuinely human life means, then to think of death as the dissolution of the body while the soul lives on untouched cannot be entirely comforting, and it would make almost inexplicable Christian hope for the resurrection of the dead.

Unsurprisingly, therefore, Christians have sometimes struggled to explain how it is that the souls of believers can be happy after death, how prior to the general resurrection they can fully flourish if separated from the body. In the *Summa Theologiae* (I/II, q. 4, a. 5, ad. 5) St. Thomas addresses the question directly, though I at least am not sure what to make of his response. As he does so often, Thomas seeks to divide and clarify the question. On the one hand, the souls of the saints in heaven see God, a vision that does not depend on bodily senses but that provides everything a created soul could desire. In this sense perfect happiness does not require the presence of the body. But on the other hand, although the desire of the separated soul is fully satisfied and at rest, possessing the good it desires, from another angle we can say that "it does not possess that good in every way [i.e., bodily] that it would wish to possess it. Consequently, after the body has been resumed, Happiness increases not in intensity, but in extent."

I confess to not finding this especially helpful, but Richard Neuhaus, attempting mightily to make good use of it, offered an imaginative way to understand St. Thomas's point. Even though the separated soul is entirely at rest and fully satisfied in the beatific vision, still, Neuhaus suggests, it "desires the body to share the joy. It is just a little like a very happy traveler sending a postcard to a friend, 'Wish you were here.'" Whether this is a helpful analogy, I have my doubts. It may be better simply to admit that, living for now as those who are always on the way but do not yet rest in the peace of Jesus, we can only say that the risen Lord has taken the departed saints into his keeping and will one day bid them rise from sleep.

Hence, rather than beginning with an anthropology (of soul and body, inner and outer, material and spiritual) that may eventually leave as many questions unanswered as answered, perhaps we should begin from the heart of Christian faith. Those who have died in Christ may be, as St. Paul writes in 2 Corinthians, "away from the body," but they are "at home with the Lord." No longer beset by "fighting without and fear within," they are at peace. And because the Lord with whom they are at home is the resurrected Christ, the Living One, they too must somehow live in him. Quite rightly, therefore, even now week after week in the Eucharist we offer our praise (in the words of the 1928 *Book of Common Prayer*) "with Angels and Archangels, and with all the company of heaven." Or, to put it in the language of the Letter to the Hebrews, we "have come to Mount Zion and to the city of the living God, the heavenly Jerusalem, and to innumerable angels in festal gathering, and to the assembly of the first-born who are enrolled in heaven, and to a judge who is God of all, and to the spirit of just men made perfect, and to Jesus. . . ."

For now, then, as we live toward our dying, we wait in hope for the great day of resurrection still to come. If we die before that day comes, we will rest in the peace of Jesus, trusting that on "a morning bright and fair" he will "bid us rise from sleep" to share with all who have hoped in him that joyous "hour of waking."

BIBLIOGRAPHY

Figgis, J. N. *The Political Aspects of St. Augustine's "City of God"*. London: Longmans, Green, 1921.

Jonas, Hans. "The Burden and Blessing of Mortality." *The Hastings Center Report* 22 (1992) 34–40.

Neuhaus, Richard John. *As I Lay Dying: Meditations upon Returning*. New York: Basic Books, 2002.

Pelikan, Jaroslav. *The Shape of Death: Life, Death, and Immortality in the Early Fathers*. Nashville: Abingdon, 1961.

Pieper, Josef. *Happiness and Contemplation*. South Bend, IN: St. Augustine's Press, 1998.

Scheffler, Samuel. *Death and the Afterlife*. Oxford: Oxford University Press, 2013.

Tolstoy, Leo. *The Death of Ivan Ilyich*. New York: Bantam Classic, 1981.

Wheelock, John Hall. "Song on Reaching Seventy." In *Songs of Experience: An Anthology of Literature on Growing Old*, edited by Margaret Fowler and Priscilla McCutcheon, 20–21. New York: Ballantine, 1991.

IV

Thinking Theologically:
To Be a Person

13

An Ecumenism of Time[1]

Almost forty years ago, having completed my General Exams, I was ready to set to work on a dissertation. Contemplating possible topics, I toyed with the idea of writing on the love of friendship. I knew of almost no contemporary scholar—with the exception of Ralph Potter—who seemed at the time to be giving much thought to the subject, and I was tempted to take a topic that seemed to be on almost no one else's radar screen. But the literature on friendship was very diffuse, it wasn't clear to me that I could successfully draw it together into a workable dissertation, and I was mindful that part of the point of a dissertation is to finish it. So I saved that topic and returned to it a few years later.

When I returned to it, and eventually wrote a little book on the subject, I still felt I was doing something quite unusual—something nobody else was thinking about. Over time I realized how mistaken that was. The truth is that other people also seemed to have developed an interest in friendship and related topics at just about the time I had. There were thinkers—some feminists, some others—defending the ideas of partiality and "care." There were critics of consequentialism defending a distinction between agent-neutral and agent-relative reasons. And there was renewed interest in Aristotle, including quite specifically his understanding of friendship.

---

1. An earlier version of this essay appeared in the *Journal of the Society of Christian Ethics* 34.2 (Fall/Winter 2014).

In other words, although I thought I had an original, creative idea, it was in fact in the air I was breathing in at the time. It turned out that quite a few people were thinking about questions I thought only I had discerned. Gradually it struck me that there was a lesson to be learned from this, and I have tried not to forget it.

Every age has its characteristic outlook. Every age is likely to see certain truths clearly and is just as likely to have certain blind spots. Even when we disagree among ourselves, we may actually share many assumptions that would have seemed far from obvious to those in other times and places. As C. S. Lewis once put it, we don't try to learn from those of other ages because they knew more than we or were more intelligent than we are. They had as many blind spots and made as many mistakes as we do. But, Lewis noted, not the same mistakes. Hence, we can learn from them. They were not parochial in the same way we are parochial.

And we *are* parochial—which, strangely enough, is one of the reasons we need to work within a tradition of thought, attempting to retrieve from it truths and insights that we do not take in with the air we breathe from the surrounding culture. Being up to date and being out of date are, after all, closely related phenomena. Accepting the discipline of thinking with those who have shaped the tradition of Christian thought offers a kind of deliverance from the narrowness of our own time and place.

Doing this is practicing what we might call an ecumenism of time. A truly ecumenical spirit involves more than a capacity to appreciate the others around us or to delight in the diversity of voices in the neighborhoods of work, home, and polity we currently inhabit. It involves a willingness to enter into conversation with those who have preceded us in the faith, to try to learn from them, and, even, to be willing to be questioned by them. It means that we think of ourselves as engaged in a shared endeavor with them.

An ecumenism of time, which begins with the tradition in which we stand, need not be narrow or sectarian in any simple sense. That depends entirely on the nature of our tradition. Peter Brown, the great historian of late antiquity, has suggested that the attraction and power of Christianity in the age of Constantine was the way it overcame the fragmentation of a polytheistic world in which those of different cultures gloried in their diversity. What would have struck a contemporary person at the time of Constantine, Brown writes, was that the Christian church was unlike the many trade associations and cultic brotherhoods which proliferated in the Roman cities. These tended to be class- or gender-specific. Fellow-craftsmen would gather with their equals to dine and worship. Women alone would form societies for the worship of their goddess. The Christian church, by contrast, was a variegated group. In that respect, it was not unlike a miniature version of the new empire.

What, then, are the advantages and the drawbacks of situating ourselves within that Christian tradition of inquiry?

WORKING WITHIN A TRADITION

Thinking within a tradition, even one with as many different strands as the Christian tradition, is a little like learning to speak one's native tongue. We first learned to speak not by being taught rules of grammar and syntax but by being immersed in and surrounded by words, by being spoken to. We did not compare the language we learned to speak with other, alternative possibilities, as if we were trying to decide whether it was superior in beauty, or in the precision of speech it made possible, or in the range of subjects its vocabulary enabled us to discuss. We simply learned how to think and communicate within it.

When our thought has been formed and structured in this way we reap certain obvious benefits. Most obvious, I suppose, is the stability it offers, but a more important aspect, not unrelated to that stability, is the depth and nuance it makes possible. Contrary to what we may sometimes suppose, working within a tradition is anything but stale and rote—at least not for anyone actually interested in thinking. Just as the best conversation takes place among friends who share fundamental beliefs while disagreeing on lots of particular questions, so our theological and ethical discussions will be liveliest and most enriching when they explore the inner workings of a way of life and thought that we share and do not for the moment need to defend. It will have the added benefit that we will not be seduced into supposing that our ideas are more original or creative than they really are.

Our first conversation partners, therefore, though by no means our only ones, must be those who have shaped the moral tradition that is now ours. It is worth remembering that for much of their history Christians did not think of ethics as a discipline separate from theology. That is why Barth argued in such rich detail that Christian ethics could not simply be a continuation or development of any general conception of ethics but must be peculiar, distinctive, and singular. Likewise, centuries earlier, Augustine had—only slightly less aggressively than Barth—suggested that Christians convert to their own use the truths of the philosophers, just as the Israelites had, at God's command, taken the Egyptian gold. When, then, we think of ourselves as standing and working within the Christian tradition, ethics simply specifies the part of the theological task that tries to discern what faithfulness should mean for people who trust that in Jesus God has been faithful to his creation.

That those who share our tradition should be our first conversation partners does not mean that we speak with no one else. Our model might be something like the way Stefan Reif once described Jonathan Sacks, formerly Chief Rabbi in Britain of the Orthodox Jewish communities—as one of those "who 'warm themselves with the coals of Torah,' but are not averse to the odd bit of central heating from secular sources." Likewise, *Lumen Fidei*, the first encyclical of Pope Francis (though an encyclical written by "four hands," his own and those of Benedict XVI, as Francis put it), though directed primarily to the faithful, finds occasion to refer in passing to Nietzsche, Rousseau, Buber, Wittgenstein, the novels of Dostoyevsky and the poetry of T. S. Eliot. More centrally, it calls attention at several points to the dialogue with Hellenistic culture that lies at the heart of the Bible. Were we to reject or ignore the insight to be gained from a variety of conversation partners, the drawbacks of locating ourselves within a tradition might well outweigh the advantages. And, in fact, working within a tradition does have its dangers, which I do not wish to overlook. In particular, it is worth our noting briefly how it may endanger freedom—both our own and our recognition of God's.

We are finite creatures, located in time and place, but we are also to some extent free. If we forget, ignore, or doubt our capacity to transcend our historical location and find some common moral ground with those whose location is very different, we underplay the importance of human freedom. So we might expect that aspects of Christian moral vision will be shared with others who do not share our faith. The Decalogue, for example, has often been read by Christians as pointing to aspects of the Christian way of life that are also essential elements in almost any shared, common life. Few societies can survive without attending to the bond between parents and children, the bond that unites husband and wife, the bond of life with life, the bond that connects persons with their possessions, and the bond by which speech manifests the speaker.

At the same time, there will be other aspects of the Christian way of life that may be more singular and particular. It is hard to imagine that self-sacrificial action would not be highly esteemed in a faith that has a crucified God at its center. Without the emphasis on the steadfast love of God for Israel and the commitment even to the point of death of that God in Jesus, we might be less likely to understand the marriage of a man and a woman as a covenant of lifelong fidelity rather than a three-year contract with an option for renewal. Without a deep belief that we are bodies made by God from the dust of the ground, we might be less inclined to think of children as a manifestation of the fleshly unity of those who beget them and more willing to think of children simply as products of the will, created by whatever techniques may be available.

Thus, we are shaped by the faith that is ours, and it has its own, singular and peculiar, character. But that singularity can make place for generality; it can open up space for insights and commitments that are shared with others. Although we are not free-floating philosophers of the moral life, we are adherents to a way of life that understands itself in mission to the world—and cannot, therefore, simply close off that world which does not yet know or speak the language of praise to the God of Abraham, Isaac, and Jacob, and the Father of Jesus.

Those who regularly recite the first article of the Apostles' or the Nicene Creed should anticipate that others we meet would share with us some common bonds, that to some extent we would be able to "translate" each other's way of life and understand each other. Thus Augustine in his *City of God*, following the lead of St. Paul in a famous speech to "men of Athens," read the story of creation: "God created man as one individual; but that did not mean that he was to remain alone, bereft of human society. God's intention was that in this way the unity of human society and the bonds of human sympathy be more emphatically brought home to man, if men were bound together not merely by likeness in nature but also by the feeling of kinship."

Hence, to practice an ecumenism of time, to work within our tradition need not undermine our freedom to seek common moral ground, when it is available, with others. In important ways, in fact, it undergirds our freedom, for it forms and shapes us as people who are not so parochial as to suppose that even ideas which first strike us as quaint or outdated have nothing to teach us.

There is also a second danger that may lie near at hand when we seek to practice an ecumenism of time and work within the Christian tradition of thought. Placing ourselves within our tradition might seem to endanger not only our freedom but also our recognition of God's freedom. Josef Pieper nicely stated the problem: "In no epoch, no matter how 'Christian' it may have been, have faith and hope been so readily available to man that he has had only to reach out for them. That is an inexorable fact; it may be forgotten, but it cannot be altered, however much we are on a familiar footing with the divine Mystery in our speech and thought."

Pieper's point is an important one for Christian thinkers. Whatever may or may not be true of other traditions of inquiry, Christian faith is not a way of life that can be confidently handed on as if it were our possession. Whatever exactly retrieval of our tradition means, it cannot mean that. The community that lives by retrieving and renewing *this* tradition does not sustain itself or its way of life; it is sustained by the free grace of God. And if we assume that God's steadfastness does not mean God simply repeating himself world without end, then it seems right to assume that our retrieval must always be a selective one. We reclaim what our predecessors in the faith saw more clearly than we, and, equally important, we honor God's freedom to correct the wrong turnings that we or those who came before us in the faith have taken.

Hence, working within a tradition does not mean that our present moment is simply dominated by the heavy hand of the past. Quite the contrary. It is we who turn to the past to make use of its resources to meet our present needs. As Servais Pinckaers says of Aquinas, "Can one not say that through his dialogue with Aristotle, Thomas has become a contemporary of the Philosopher, or, if you will, that he has introduced him into his own age, and into the University of Paris, as a contemporary master? Can one not likewise think that Aristotle and Thomas may become our contemporaries . . . ?" We treat our ancestors in the faith as people who are not irrelevant to our own deepest questions and concerns. We learn from them, to be sure; we also engage with them and even cannibalize their ideas as we pursue our own purposes and develop our own vision.

Perhaps it is worth noting that in making these general observations about the advantages and the drawbacks of working within a tradition, I have, in fact, been doing just that. I have been thinking within Christian terms that depict human beings as two-sided creatures, finite and free, made from the dust of the ground but made also to transcend time and place in order finally to rest in God. About each one of these human beings there is something deeply mysterious, a mystery that we mark by calling them "persons," and I want now to turn from these general reflections to a more particular act of retrieval by thinking about what it means to call someone a person. It is, after all, in our cultural history, a Christian word. Retrieving some of its significance may give us reason to question some of the ways we have come, in more recent times, to think about what it means to be a person.

PERSONS

It is rarely a bad idea to begin an act of Christian retrieval with St. Augustine, and I start therefore with just two passages from his treatise on the Trinity. Noting that the language of three persons might seem to suggest three individual substances or three gods, he writes, "[S]ince the Father is only called so because he has a Son, and the Son is only called so because he has a Father, these things are not said substance-wise, as neither is said with reference to itself but only with reference to the other. . . . Therefore, although being Father is different from being Son, there is no difference of substance, because they are not called these things substance-wise but relationship-wise." That is to say, the distinction between Father and Son is one of relation, not of characteristics or qualities. Or, again, just slightly later, Augustine makes a closely related point quite straightforwardly: "So, then, the Father is almighty, the Son is almighty, the Holy Spirit is almighty; yet there are not three almighties but one almighty."

The second of these passages ought to call to mind its verbal echo in the third of the ecumenical creeds, commonly known as the Athanasian Creed, though almost surely not written by Athanasius and produced a century or so later than Augustine. Recall its rhythmic stanzas. Uncreated is the Father; uncreated is the Son; uncreated is the Spirit. The Father is infinite, the Son infinite, the Holy Spirit infinite. The Father eternal, the Son eternal, the Holy Spirit eternal. "Yet there are not three eternals, but one eternal; just as there are not three increates or three infinites, but one increate and one infinite."

Thus, with respect to any quality or capacity we ascribe to one of the three persons, the same must be ascribed to each of the other two. We cannot distinguish among the three persons by pointing to any qualities or capacities. Nonetheless, we must distinguish them. We do so only in terms of the relations that mark their shared history. "The Father is from none, not made nor created nor begotten. The Son is from the Father alone, not made nor created but begotten. The Holy Spirit is from the Father and the Son, not made nor created nor begotten but proceeding. . . . And in this Trinity there is nothing before or after, nothing greater or less, but all three persons are coeternal with each other and coequal."

If we try our best to practice an ecumenism of time—and we are, after all, here at the very heart of Christian belief in God, however diminished in contemporary Christian consciousness Trinitarian dogma may have become—what, then, does it mean to speak of a person? Robert Spaemann has recently developed the point with philosophical care. Put most simply, a person is a "someone," not a "something." Not a something marked by certain properties, but a someone marked by a history in relation. "*Who* we are is not simply interchangeable with *what* we are."

Fully committed Jewish monotheists that the first followers of Jesus were, they had to think through the fact that they were something more than just "followers." After all, they prayed to Jesus and worshiped him. They spoke of him as having been sent by his Father, the God of Israel, and as having promised to send a Spirit who would continue his own presence in the world. So they believed in one God but told a story that gave them three ways to name that God. They needed to distinguish the three persons without undermining their equality but also without retracting the monotheism to which they were committed.

Trinitarian teaching, laboriously worked out over time, was the result. The three persons—Father, Son, Spirit—are *numerically* but not *qualitatively* distinct. That is, we cannot distinguish them from each other by any capacities they individually possess. They are distinguished only in terms of their relations to one another. Hence, the Son is not *different from* the Father or the Spirit, but *other than* the Father and the Spirit.

Almost simultaneously, Christians were trying to decide what they wanted or needed to say about Jesus. He was clearly a human being, and it was important to them that he was. He ate, drank, slept, lived in a particular time and place, wept, suffered, died. But, of course, they also worshiped him as one whose nature was divine—the lord of life and death, the God of Abraham and Caesar, the ruler and judge of history. They thought of him, that is, as characterized by properties that were human and properties that were divine. Was he some third kind of entity—a god and a man (each with its own characteristic qualities) glued together?

On this question also the Athanasian Creed distinguishes the language of persons from that of natures and their qualities. Jesus, it says, exists fully as God and fully as a human being, "composed of a rational soul and human flesh, equal to the Father in respect of his divinity, less than the Father in respect of his humanity." How is this possible? Well, of course, it is mysterious, but it happens "not by the transformation of his divinity into flesh, but by the taking up of his humanity into God." Hence, Jesus is said to be completely one in the unity of his person without any confusion of the two natures.

To be sure, this essentially Chalcedonian solution, if we want to call it a solution, is not without its difficulties. Someone else, attempting to retrieve our tradition on another occasion, might wish to pursue them. For my purposes it is important simply to note, again, what this means for our understanding of persons. In order to say what they thought they needed to say about Jesus, Christians distinguished between *what we have* (that is, our nature, with its properties and capacities) and *who we are* (our person). Of course, there is something mysterious here, for each person—each one of us—is mysterious. Augustine would not have disagreed. "When," he writes in *The Trinity*, "you ask 'Three what?' human speech labors under a great dearth of words. So we say three persons, not in order to say that precisely, but in order not to be reduced to silence." Each person is marked by what the philosopher John Crosby has characterized as an "incommunicability" or an "unrepeatability." Those who knew and loved Socrates, Crosby writes,

> will insist that there was in Socrates something absolutely unrepeatable, they will say that there was a mystery of the man and that Socrates was not a mere instance or specimen of this mystery but that he *was* this mystery, so that a second Socrates is strictly, absolutely impossible. When Socrates died, a hole was left in the world, such that no subsequent person could possibly fill it.

Perhaps the point can be made more engagingly if we turn away from theologians and philosophers to one who knew a little of each but, more important, had thought his way into a Christian understanding of persons. G. K. Chesterton wrote of

> a certain instinctive attitude which feels the things in which all men agree to be unspeakably important, and all the things in which they differ (such as mere brains) to be almost unspeakably

unimportant. The nearest approach to it in our ordinary life would be the promptitude with which we should consider mere humanity in any circumstance of shock or death. We should say, after a somewhat disturbing discovery, "There is a dead man under the sofa." We should not be likely to say, "There is a dead man of considerable personal refinement under the sofa." We should say, "A woman has fallen into the water." We should not say, "A highly educated woman has fallen into the water." Nobody would say, "There are the remains of a clear thinker in your back garden." Nobody would say, "Unless you hurry up and stop him, a man with a very fine ear for music will have jumped off that cliff."

At any rate, this is an understanding of what it means to be a person that deeply shaped our tradition. To be sure, it is not the only understanding. It differs from Boethius's famous definition of a person as an "individual substance of a rational nature." However, my retrieval has been deliberately selective, an attempt to get at what seems to me to be at the very heart of the tradition.

We are not persons because we have certain capacities. Being a person is much more inward and mysterious than that. Were it a matter of capacities, some of us would have more "personhood," some of us little or none at all—and then, perhaps, only with great difficulty could we avoid assuming that some of us are of greater worth or value than others of us.

PERSONS OR PERSONHOOD

The story of the last half-century—most especially, perhaps, in ethical thought about the beginning and the end of life—is a story of the diminishment of this understanding of persons that I have attempted to retrieve. Where we might have built on the insight handed down to us in our tradition, where we might have used it to better and deepen the way the tradition itself has thought about persons, we have taken our cues from elsewhere. We might almost say, for example, that bioethics took a wrong turn from the moment of its birth. It was in 1972, in the second volume of *The Hastings Center Report*, that Joseph Fletcher published his "Indicators of Humanhood: A Tentative Profile of Man." Although the language was at that time still somewhat fluid, his aim was to distinguish between the class of human beings and the narrower class of persons. Among the "indicators" he took seriously were self-awareness and self-control (lacking which, as he put it, one has a life "about on a par with a paramecium"). Apart from cortical function, he wrote, "the *person* is non-existent."

It was primarily, I suspect, in discussions of abortion that the difference between "person" (who we are) and "personhood" (capacities we may or may not have) was blurred and largely lost. If we look back at the essays, many of them classics in the genre, published in a book that was once a staple in many ethics classes—*The Problem of Abortion*, edited by Joel Feinberg—we will find that much of the time no particular difference between "person" and "personhood" is in evidence. And whatever the language used, it is generally a matter of the presence or absence of certain capacities or qualities that is thought to be important. The "crucial question," as Michael Tooley put it, is this: "At what point does a developing human being acquire the concept of a continuing self, and at what point is it capable of having an interest in its own continued existence?" Or, similarly, in her oft-reprinted essay "On the Moral and Legal Status of Abortion," Mary Anne Warren, distinguishing between genetic humanity and moral humanity, wrote, "The suggestion is simply that the moral community consists of all and only *people*, rather than all and only human beings; and probably the best way of demonstrating its self-evidence is by considering the concept of personhood, to see what sorts of entity are and are not persons."

Quite naturally, similar understandings, focusing on what we have rather than who we are, migrated from the beginning to the end of life. Thus, for example, with respect to people whose capacities are greatly diminished and who are in need of medical care, we began to distinguish different senses of "futility" in treatment. Medical treatment was "quantitatively" futile if it probably could not preserve life for very long. It was "qualitatively" futile if, for example, it preserved continued life of the biological organism but without consciousness of one's self. This slide from thinking of persons to thinking of personhood has been going on for as long as I have been reading, thinking, and writing about moral problems that arise at the beginning and the end of life.

We have too often lost the mysterious sense of the person—of the person's incommunicability, inwardness, and unrepeatability—that is integral to a Christian understanding of the triune God. Losing it, we then go in search of a different understanding, which generally turns out to focus on some set of properties, qualities, or capacities, the unequal distribution of which inevitably endangers the equal dignity of human persons.

To be sure, acknowledging the mystery of the person does not mean ignoring the biological organism with its qualities, capacities, and distinctive marks. A Christian understanding of persons cannot be divorced from the context of the created nature that we share. Only there, in the body, do we come to know each other as persons. The body is the place of our personal presence, not however because its capacities mark the presence of the person, but because the biological is taken up—assumed—into the person, even as the human nature of Jesus is taken up into his person.

If we begin to retrieve our tradition's understanding, we will not make comparative assessments of the "personhood" of our fellow human beings. Instead, we will try to school ourselves (not to assess, but) to "recognize" others as persons—as someone, not something. Our approach should be a little like that described by Kierkegaard when he invites us to suppose that

> there are two artists and one of them says, "I have traveled much and seen much in the world, but I have sought in vain to find a person worth painting. I have found no face that was the perfect image of beauty to such a degree that I could decide to sketch it; in every face I have seen one or another little defect, and therefore I seek in vain." Would this be a sign that this artist is a great artist? The other artist, however, says, "Well, I do not actually profess to be an artist; I have not traveled abroad either but stay at home with the little circle of people who are closest to me, since I have not found one single face to be so insignificant or so faulted that I still could not discern a more beautiful side and discover something transfigured in it. That is why, without claiming to be an artist, I am happy in the art I practice and find it satisfying." Would this not be a sign that he is indeed the artist, he who by bringing a certain something with him found right on the spot what the well-traveled artist did not find anywhere in the world—perhaps because he did not bring a certain something with him! Therefore the second of the two would be the artist.

Indeed, if we do not bring that "certain something" with us in our dealings with others, I wonder whether they can really develop the qualities and capacities we prize so highly. As Robert Spaemann put it, "The mother, or her substitute, treats the child from the start as a subject of personal encounter rather than an object to manipulate or a living organism to condition. She teaches the child to speak, not by speaking in its presence but by speaking *to* it." That is, she draws the child into relation with her, into their shared history. She does not first cultivate certain qualities in the child until at some point that little something becomes a someone qualified to share with her a history.

Now, to be sure, there may be no certain way to demonstrate that we must "recognize" each of our fellow human beings as a someone, a person, whatever capacities they may possess or may lack. The ability and the willingness so to open ourselves to the call of another person is an invitation we can refuse. But to do so is to undermine the gift of equal personal dignity that our tradition has bequeathed to us.

If that gift has too often been absent from our world, we should not blame the absence on others. It is our own doing, and we are in need of a great act of retrieval. We are not just members of a species or instances of a universal type, and the nature we have must be distinguished from the person we are. As the late Ralph McInerny, a discerning Christian philosopher, noted,

> The point of a proper name is that it [is] not common to many, and yet many people do bear identical names. . . . But even when two persons have the same proper name it does not become a common noun, like "man." All the John Smiths that have been, are, and will be have nothing in common but the name; it does not name something common to them all. There is an inescapable nominalism here. God calls us all by our proper name, and He is unlikely to confuse one John Smith with another.

For those called to practice an ecumenism of time, the task is to go and do likewise.

BIBLIOGRAPHY

Augustine, Saint. *The Trinity*. Translated by Edmund Hill. Brooklyn: New City, 1991.

Brown, Peter. *The Rise of Western Christendom: Triumph and Diversity, A.D. 200–1000*. 2nd ed. Malden, MA: Blackwell, 2003.

Chesterton, G. K. *The Collected Works of G. K. Chesterton I: Heretics; Orthodoxy; The Blatchford Controversies*. San Francisco: Ignatius, 1986.

Crosby, John F. *Personalist Papers*. Washington, DC: Catholic University of America Press, 2003.

———. "The Twofold Source of the Dignity of Persons." *Faith and Philosophy* 18 (2001) 292–306.

Feinberg, Joel, ed. *The Problem of Abortion*. Belmont, CA: Wadsworth, 1973.

Kierkegaard, Søren. *Works of Love*. Translated by Howard V. Hong and Edna H. Hong. Princeton: Princeton University Press, 1995.

Pieper, Josef. *Scholasticism: Personalities and Problems of Medieval Philosophy*. New York: McGraw-Hill, 1964.

Pinckaers, Servais-Théodore. "The Sources of the Ethics of St. Thomas Aquinas." In *The Ethics of Aquinas*, edited by Stephen J. Pope, 17–29. Washington, DC: Georgetown University Press, 2002.

Reif, Stefan C. "Jewish Authority." *Times Literary Supplement*, August 2, 2013.

Spaemann, Robert. *Persons: The Difference between "Someone" and "Something"*. Translated by Oliver O'Donovan. Oxford: Oxford University Press, 2006.

14

The "Unrepeatability" of Persons[1]

The principle of utility, at least as it is commonly used in ethical theorizing, is framed in terms of aggregate goods—promoting the greatest good for the greatest number of people. By contrast, the dignity bestowed on persons because of their relation to God is inherently individualizing. As the late Ralph McInerny once wrote,

> The point of a proper name is that it [is] not common to many, and yet many people do bear identical names. . . . But even when two persons have the same proper name it does not become a common noun, like "man." All the John Smiths that have been, are, and will be have nothing in common but the name; it does not name something common to them all. There is an inescapable nominalism here. God calls us all by our proper name, and He is unlikely to confuse one John Smith with another.

This contrast—between the aggregating nature of utility and the individualizing nature of dignity—lies at the heart of some of the questions that most trouble us when we think about how we ought to live.

We name the particular, unrepeatable

---

1. Excerpted and revised from *Why People Matter*, edited by John F. Kilner, copyright © 2017. Used by permission of Baker Academic, a division of Baker Publishing Group.

SIDGWICK AND THE DUALISM OF PRACTICAL REASON

One need not be, like McInerny, a Christian philosopher in order to sense the problem. For example, Henry Sidgwick, though little known today outside professional philosophy circles, was one of the most influential British moral philosophers in the last half of the nineteenth century. His book, *The Methods of Ethics*, on which he labored for years and which went through seven (always carefully revised) editions, is still today one of the classic texts in the tradition of utililtarian thought.

Perhaps strangely, however, although the *Methods* attends to most of the issues that have been important for utilitarian ethics, it is actually dominated by a somewhat different problem—what Sidgwick called "the dualism of practical reason." Utilitarians think that when we act we are aiming to produce happiness. For Sidgwick, happiness was reducible to pleasure, but some utilitarians have held that there are other ways of determining the greatest good for human life. At any rate, Sidgwick thought that we should aim to produce the greatest aggregate happiness possible. But, of course, someone else might take a different view, believing that I should aim at my *individual* happiness, rather than the aggregate *general* happiness. Hence, Sidgwick recognized two forms of hedonism, which he called egoistic and universalistic hedonism. The universal form of hedonism was utilitarianism, the theory to which Sidgwick was committed. But he acknowledged that it might not be irrational for a person to pursue his own happiness rather than the general happiness.

Practical reason seems, then, to speak with two voices. On the one hand, Sidgwick argues at length that it is reasonable for us to seek the happiness of the larger whole ("the universe of sentient beings") to which we belong. But, on the other hand, it is also reasonable for us to act in whatever way is most conducive to our own happiness. These two voices cannot be reconciled, or so Sidgwick thought. Utilitarian though he was, and believing as he did that it is our obligation to pursue the greatest happiness for the greatest number, he nevertheless held that ethical egoism was not an irrational position to hold. Why he should have thought this, given his utilitarian commitments, is, as his biographer, Bart Schultz, puts it, "one of the most important and puzzling problems arising out of over a century of commentary on the *Methods*."

Sidgwick was the son of a clergyman, but as a young man he had experienced a crisis of faith. He remained wistfully eager to believe but unable to do so—to the degree that John Maynard Keynes is supposed to have said of him, "He never did anything but wonder whether Christianity was true and prove it wasn't and hope that it was." It may well, I suspect, have been the lingering vestiges of Christian belief that made it so difficult for Sidgwick simply to dismiss the claims of the self and subordinate them to the general happiness. An important passage in the *Methods* emphasizes the distinctive significance of individual persons: "It would be contrary to Common Sense to deny that the distinction between any one individual and any other is real and fundamental, and that consequently 'I' am concerned with the quality of my existence as an individual in a sense, fundamentally important, in which I am not concerned with the quality of the existence of other individuals." Were persons simply parts of a single whole, this dualism would vanish. But it was impossible to think of persons that way so long as the remnants of Christian belief continued to shape his thinking.

This was the reason, Bart Schultz believes, that Sidgwick discerned in moral reasoning "a potentially explosive contradiction, waiting to emerge, once the religious worldview fades. Put differently, Sidgwick questions, in a way that other secular utilitarians did not, the degree to which the utilitarian evolution of morality may in fact, perhaps paradoxically, have depended on the evolution of Christianity." The problem, at least in Sidgwick's mind, was a simple one, and it consumed much of his intellectual energy throughout his life. If the world could no longer be believed to be one in which God would ultimately honor the distinctive dignity of each individual, what possible reason could there be for not simply pursuing one's own good here and now?

Sidgwick spent many of his adult years investigating the claims of parapsychology. He was a founder and first president of the Society for Psychical Research, formed in 1882, engaging with others in, as Schultz so aptly puts it, "an endeavor to reenchant the universe." The sober philosopher found himself consulting mediums at séances. He engaged in careful study of telepathy (that is, transferring information from one person to another in some way other than through any of our normal sensory channels). He had a deep interest in reports of ghosts and haunted houses.

Why? Why was he so committed to this research? Because he needed evidence of an "Afterlife" if the universe were to be reenchanted. For if the universe lacked moral order, if utilitarian virtue that aimed at the aggregate good of all sentient beings were to go unrewarded, no one could say that it was irrational for individual persons to promote as best they could their own individual good.

"Rational to promote common good"

That was Sidgwick's problem: He was committed to a utilitarian theory that seemed to lose the distinctiveness of individuals in its search for an aggregate good. That distinctiveness might once have been defended in Christian terms, and those terms held just enough sway over Sidgwick that he could not discount the fundamental moral significance of each individual person, even though he no longer pictured the world in Christian terms. The only remaining defenders of individual distinctiveness were those who asserted that one's own good rather than an aggregate good ought to be a person's aim. Given his vestigial commitment to individual distinctiveness, Sidgwick could not claim that their egoistic view was contrary to reason. Yet, given his commitment to utilitarianism, Sidgwick also regarded pursuit of the general good as reasonable and right. Hence, the dualism of practical reason.

CHRISTIANITY AND INDIVIDUAL DISTINCTIVENESS

For Christians the defense of individual distinctiveness over against aggregate utility will necessarily take a different shape. Sidgwick's problem was that he could find no answer for those who asserted the reasonableness of seeking to maximize one's own individual good. But those who believe, as St. Paul writes in Colossians, that their life is "hid with Christ in God" should be freed from the temptation to suppose that they need to seek their own happiness. Hence, for Christians, utilitarianism will be problematic for different reasons, especially two that may be expressed as questions. Do we wrong others in any way if we regard them simply as parts of a larger whole whose aggregate good we seek? Do we wrong ourselves in any way if we think of ourselves simply as agents in service of promoting a general good? As a way to express the wrongs we might do to others or ourselves if we think solely in terms of promoting aggregate utility, the language of dignity has increasingly been used, and, after briefly characterizing our human nature, I will return to these questions about utility and dignity.

For Christians to explore these topics requires that we think about what we might call the strange two-sidedness of our creaturely nature. In *The Magician's Nephew*, sixth in the Chronicles of Narnia series, C. S. Lewis imaginatively depicts this. The great lion Aslan creates the land of Narnia and its inhabitants. In the course of doing so, he sets apart some animals as Talking Beasts, the primary inhabitants of Narnia. "He was going to and fro among the animals. And every now and then he would go up to two of them (always two at a time) and touch their noses with his." These animals "instantly left their own kinds and followed him," while the others wandered away. Then Aslan breathes on the chosen ones and, in the "deepest, wildest voice" the children had ever heard, says, "Narnia, Narnia, Narnia, awake. Love. Think. Speak. . . . Be talking beasts." That these are *talking* beasts points to something more. "Creatures," says Aslan, "I give you yourselves." They are no longer simply instinctive creatures. They can be other than they are, distancing themselves from themselves—for that is what it means that they are given themselves.

Lewis is here depicting imaginatively a distinctive feature of human life, as Christians have understood it. Christians have learned to think of human beings as complex creatures, located in time and place but simultaneously able to transcend that location at least in thought. "Man's involvement in finiteness and his transcendence over it" is, Reinhold Niebuhr once suggested, "the basic paradox of human existence."

A simple, if unlikely, illustration is one I have often used to explicate what Niebuhr characterizes as a paradox. If I fall from the top of a fifty-story building, the law of gravity takes over, just as it does if we drop a rock from that building; for we are finite beings, located in space and time and subject to natural necessity. Nevertheless, we are also free and able, at least to some extent, to transcend the limits of nature and history. Therefore, as I fall from that building, there are truths about my experience that could not be captured by any explanation in terms of mass and velocity. Something different happens in my fall than in the rock's fall, for *this* falling object is also a subject characterized by self-awareness. I can know myself as a falling object, which means that I can to some degree "distance" myself from that object. Hence, I both am and am not that falling object. I cannot simply be equated with it. I am that object and am free from it, freed by my capacity to transcend it.

We can, no doubt, imagine a being who is pure spirit—an angel, say, or the god of the philosophers. We can also imagine a being who is entirely limited to the body—whose *anima*, whose life principle, has no capacity to transcend the limits of nature and history.

When we think of a human being, however, we have to think of one who is neither pure self-transcending spirit nor simply finite body—but, somehow, the union of both. Quite often Christians have expressed this by saying that the human person is a union of body and soul. True as that may be, when we try to articulate its meaning, we often think of such a person as a composite of two things that are in principle separable—temporarily glued together in this life but destined to be separated in such a way that the person lives on after the body has died—and that will one day perhaps, by God's grace, be reunited in the resurrection.

That picture is likely to lead us astray when thinking of human dignity, for it necessarily invites us to think in dualistic ways and tempts us to reduce the "real" person in the end to either just body or just soul. A somewhat different image, which I borrow from C. S. Lewis, comes closer to the truth. Think first of a rider mounted on his horse—two things temporarily joined but readily separated. But now suppose that instead of a mounted rider we imagine a centaur. In the centaur there is real union rather than a dualism that temporarily unites two essentially separate beings. With a centaur we cannot shoot the horse out from under and have the rider survive unscathed. Nor can we imagine the living horse apart from the rider, as if it were just an animal. The image of the centaur is that of a real union, an image of the union of free spirit and finite body that is the human person.

To honor the peculiar dignity of human persons—who are embodied creatures made from the dust of the ground, but who are also self-transcending creatures made for union with God—we must let our thought and action be shaped by both aspects of our being. Because persons transcend their communities, their good is not just part of an aggregate good. We may not use them or treat them merely as parts of a whole or as means to the general well-being of their communities. At the same time, we are not solely free spirits; we are finite and limited beings whose actions should recognize and acknowledge our own limits. We can briefly explore each of these constraints on any of our attempts to foster social utility.

UNDERMINING INDIVIDUAL DIGNITY

The danger that personal dignity may be undermined by the search for aggregate social utility is near at hand when we deal with issues in bioethics. For example, the enormous social (and medical) pressure to offer the "gift of life" to the sick and dying through organ donation and transplantation has invited (or tempted) us to treat human organs as a public resource that could be routinely "harvested" from the newly dead, to contemplate treating organs as commodities that could be bought or sold, and to try to expand the number of available organs by redefining death in special cases (as, for example, by simply stipulating that anencephalic newborns are dead and, hence, available as sources for organs, even when they continue to show evidence of brain stem activity).

Even more significant, perhaps, have been recurring abuses in human experimentation, one of the issues that first caused the fledgling field of bioethics to become a matter for public concern. In 1966 Dr. Henry Beecher of Harvard Medical School published in *The New England Journal of Medicine* an article with the modest title, "Ethics and Clinical Research." The article's title might have been low-key, but its contents were not. Beecher identified twenty-two instances of human experimentation that raised troubling questions about whether the dignity of the persons who were research subjects had really been honored. In the years since, some cases—such as the Tuskegee syphilis study or the human radiation experiments—have become well known as instances in which the search for medically useful knowledge was allowed to override the dignity of the persons who were research subjects. But other less well-known research from which all of us profit, such as the development of vaccines or new therapies, has sometimes used subjects (including even fetuses) who lack the ability to consent to their participation.

One of the now classic essays in bioethics, first published in 1969, was Hans Jonas's "Philosophical Reflections on Experimenting with Human Subjects." There are, Jonas believed, times when it is not just desirable but imperative that a society avoid disaster. Hence, it may conscript soldiers to fight. We do not, however, conscript experimental subjects in the "war" against disease. We value greatly the improvements to life made possible by medical research, but we have not thought of ourselves as having an obligation to produce them. That is because, although research betters our lives, it does not save our society. Because this is true, far from using those who might be most readily available as handy research subjects, we should be most reluctant to use them. Instead, Jonas defended "the inflexible principle that utter helplessness demands utter protection." If that is the right way to respect the dignity of those who are most vulnerable, we will have to ask ourselves whether it is right to build our medical progress upon the lives of those who have not given their consent or are unable to give consent.

The tension between producing good results and honoring the dignity of particular individuals also appears in the use of new reproductive technologies. Aimed at providing babies for those who are infertile, such techniques have often made use of sperm or ova provided by donors whose anonymity is protected. (Actually, of course, these people are more often vendors than donors, but the language of donation is commonly used.) As a result, however, the children produced are likely to lack significant information about their identity. The following imaginary scenario—adapted from an illustration offered by an interviewee in the documentary *Anonymous Father's Day*—makes clear how problematic it can be to treat genetic identity as insignificant.

> Mary Smith and her husband, John, are expecting the birth of their first child in a few weeks. John has a business trip that will take him briefly out of the country, and Mary would like to accompany him. Her physician says that it should be fine for her to do so, since the trip is relatively brief, and they should be back well before her due date. As long as she feels physically able to travel, her physician sees no reason why Mary should not.
>
> Two days after they arrive at the location of John's meeting, Mary goes into labor—ahead of schedule, to be sure, but not so prematurely as to threaten the child's life. And indeed, although Mary is in labor for the better part of a day, she gives birth to a baby who should survive and live a healthy life. Mary is exhausted, of course, so John stays at her bedside while she rests, and the baby is cared for by the nursing staff.
>
> A few hours later Mary feels stronger, and she and John ask to see their baby. "Certainly," says the nurse. "We'll bring you a baby right away."
>
> "Well, no," Mary replies, "we don't want to see *a* baby; we want to see *our* baby."
>
> "Oh," says the nurse, "that's not how we do things here. We make sure all the babies are doing well, and then we give you one of those babies. So it works out fine for everyone. Every family leaves with a baby whose future with them should be bright."

We know instinctively that something has gone wrong here. It is as if something important for an individual's identity could simply be discarded as we produce a well-ordered society in which everyone can flourish. But that is how a child produced through anonymous gamete donation might think about the process by which he was produced, however well he did in life. To be sure, we could retain a commitment to reproductive technology while prohibiting anonymity in gamete donation, but then donations might be considerably fewer, and many who desire to produce a child through this technology might be disappointed. We buy the happiness of others at some cost to the children produced.

These are only examples of the sorts of puzzles we face if we make aggregate utility rather than individual dignity our most fundamental moral aim. For just such reasons, at least from the time of John Stuart Mill, utilitarians have often formulated their position in terms not simply of the greatest aggregate happiness but of the greatest happiness for the greatest number—thereby attempting to incorporate an individualizing principle of distribution into their norm. This too easily obscures the question whether the good of the aggregate of all persons really is also *each* person's good. These two are not quite the same, and a search for the greatest value altogether cannot really focus on the distinction between your good and mine.

Thus, in many ways we may forget that respect for the dignity of others should serve as a kind of red light that keeps us from simply co-opting them into the service of socially useful projects, even very important ones. Each person, made for God, transcends the communities to which he or she belongs. No one's good is simply part of an aggregate good. That is one way in which honoring the dignity of persons will set limits to our pursuit of what is socially useful.

UNDERMINING LIMITS ON HUMAN AGENCY

Self-transcendence is, however, only one aspect of who we are. Because we are made to rest in God, we are not ourselves gods. As embodied human beings we are also located and limited. That simple fact, taken seriously, should keep us from inflating our responsibility for producing socially useful results, as if we could really see with the eye of the universe. It should form our sense of ourselves as moral agents who are obligated to seek socially useful ends, but obligated also to respect certain limits in that search.

Why not take organs for transplant from patients who are in a persistent vegetative state and who are therefore no longer able to interact with us, pursue any projects of their own, or be conscious of their surroundings? Why not use so-called spare embryos (from in vitro fertilization procedures) for research? (After all, since they are almost surely destined for destruction anyway, will not something be gained and nothing lost?)

We could no doubt multiply examples, but there is no need. Engaging in such practices may violate the dignity of those whom we use to accomplish our (quite possibly good) purposes. That danger, discussed above, is the first way in which a focus on utility may undermine individual dignity. There is also, however, a second issue. A willingness to engage in such activities may invite us to forget that our relation to God should place limits on the exercise of our freedom.

There may sometimes be circumstances in life when our search for the socially useful tempts us to do evil. And if we give in to that temptation, we might say, in Thomas Nagel's helpful formulation, "*things* will be better, what *happens* will be better. . . . But I will have done something worse." To give in at such moments is to lose the sense of ourselves as limited moral agents. It is as if we tried to view our action from the outside and thought of it as a choice made by someone else—a choice about what is best on the whole from the point of view of the universe. It is as if, Nagel suggests, I were asked to "decide directly among states of the world." But what sort of agent would one have to be to make such a decision, to look with the eye of the universe?

This point was nicely illustrated by the philosopher J. B. Schneewind in an article with the seemingly puzzling title, "The Divine Corporation and the History of Ethics." Schneewind sketched a way of understanding an ethic—the traditional, received Christian ethic—in which our responsibility to achieve socially useful aggregate goods is always limited. To be sure, Schneewind did this in part for the sake of explaining how modern moral philosophy had developed by turning away from that received Christian ethic. But to understand his notion of the divine corporation is to comprehend something of the concept of personal dignity as I have been using it here.

We begin by imagining our world as a cooperative endeavor created, ordered, and governed by God. In it, as in any cooperative endeavor, participants play their respective roles, carry out the tasks assigned them, and in so doing they join together to produce a good that none of them could have produced alone. No one participant is responsible for achieving the good of the whole or the best overall good possible; yet, the work of each is ordered toward that good. Sometimes individual agents will see more or less clearly how their tasks are related to the overall good. If, then, they only fulfill their assigned task and ignore altogether the general good, they would—and should—be subject to criticism. For in addition to carrying out one's individual task, each person needs to act creatively in ways that are not simply given in any role. That is part of what it means to be an agent who is not only finite but also free.

At other times, however, an individual may not be able to see the larger good his assigned duty serves. In such cases, Schneewind believes, he cannot really be criticized for ignoring the larger good while just "minding his own business," for he simply does not know that larger good. We can imagine a world—rather like our world—in which the overall good is very important but also very complex, far too complex for any individual agent always to be sure of how his work helps to produce it. And we can also imagine that the supervisor in charge of this supremely important but very complex project is able to foresee problems and deal with emergencies, is fair in his supervision, and is good—"too good ever to assign any duties that would be improper from any point of view." Such a world, imagined as a cooperative endeavor with God as that uniquely qualified supervisor, is what Schneewind calls the Divine Corporation. The dignity of individual agents who work within that Divine Corporation is closely connected to the limits on what they should attempt to do. To try simply to be all freedom, to act without limits in order to produce the aggregate good they think best, would be to picture themselves as something other—and more godlike—than human beings. It would be to suppose that they could fill the role of that uniquely qualified supervisor.

We can supplement Schneewind's workplace metaphor with a helpful literary one drawn from C. S. Lewis. Think of individuals not as agents in the Divine Corporation but as characters in a play. They know the part that has been given them, and each must play it in his own way. But none of them is the dramatist or director, and none of them is responsible for working out the play's plot satisfactorily. Something like that is our situation in life. We are not the author but characters in the story—under authority. Thus, as Lewis put it,

> We do not know the play. We do not even know whether we are in Act I or Act V. We do not know who are the major and who the minor characters. The Author knows. . . . That it has a meaning we may be sure, but we cannot see it. When it is over, we may be told. We are led to expect that the Author will have something to say to each of us on the part that each of us has played. The playing it well is what matters infinitely.

Whichever metaphor we prefer, it is clear that if God recedes as a governing, directing, authorial presence whose responsibility it is to see to the good of the whole or work out the plot of the play, it may seem that human responsibility correspondingly increases and intensifies. We may come to see ourselves as the agents whose responsibility it is to make things work out best on the whole. That is, it becomes our task to determine and achieve the greatest aggregate good. Utility displaces the dignity that marks a characteristically human—and, hence, limited—life. Hubris threatens to replace humility.

I have, of course, made this point in a way that is intended to suggest a problem with utilitarian theory—namely, the way in which it invites us to lose a sense of limits. We will not see or appreciate the lure of utilitarianism, however, unless we also acknowledge what is appealing here. Imagine a world—Sidgwick's world—in which morally serious people have lost a sense of God's providential governance. In that world, an earnest person such as Sidgwick can hardly avoid feeling the lure of utilitarianism. After all, in a world filled with suffering and terrors, we might easily suppose that those of us who remain morally serious must accept the burden of producing the best consequences possible. Even standard Christian moral language of freedom from legalism and love for those in need might be conscripted in service of accepting that burden and thereby increase the appeal of utilitarian thinking. We are easily drawn to lose a sense of our moral limits.

Still, fathers and mothers, at least in their best moments, know better; for parenthood is nothing if not a school in which we learn the limits of our ability to shape the future. John Ames, the seventy-six-year-old preacher who is the narrator of Marilynne Robinson's *Gilead* and who is writing a long letter about life to his young son, recounts a sermon he had once preached about Abraham and his sons Isaac and Ishmael. Abraham had been prepared to sacrifice Isaac at the Lord's command; Ishmael he sent off into the wilderness with his mother, Hagar. Ames reflects that "any father, particularly an old father, must finally give his child up to the wilderness and trust to the providence of God. . . . Great faith is required to give the child up, trusting God to honor the parents' love for him by assuring that there will indeed be angels in that wilderness." When we reflect upon the most significant bonds in our lives, we know that we are not and should not try to be simply agents in service of the general good. Dirty Harry speaks the truth in the movie *Magnum Force*: "A man's got to know his limitations."

INDIVIDUAL PERSONS, ALWAYS IN RELATION

In two ways, then, personal dignity is an inherently individualizing concept. It resists our inclination to think of the well-being of others chiefly in terms of aggregate social utility. And it resists our inclination to think of ourselves as if we were other than or more than limited, located agents, with a correspondingly limited responsibility for producing socially useful results through our actions. This is what it means to think of ourselves as the strange, two-sided creatures who are simultaneously located and distanced from themselves. Distinctively individual, we are not simply parts of any aggregate social whole, and faithful action on our part is not primarily aimed at producing such an aggregate good.

Perhaps, however, this forces upon us a further, important question. Is this emphasis on individual distinctiveness problematic? Is it individualistic in a way that should trouble Christians? Such questions might naturally occur to us, and it remains to consider this problem briefly. In order really to think about the dignity of persons, we need to recall the distinctively Christian understanding of what it means to be a person. And although many today may largely have forgotten this, Christians formed their notion of a person by thinking about the triune character of the God they worshiped. A brief foray into the structure of Trinitarian belief is therefore needed.

Noting that the language of three persons (in the one God) might seem to suggest three individual substances or three gods, St. Augustine wrote, "[S]ince the Father is only called so because he has a Son, and the Son is only called so because he has a Father, these things are not said substance-wise, as neither is said with reference to itself but only with reference to the other. . . . Therefore, although being Father is different from being Son, there is no difference of substance, because they are not called these things substance-wise but relationship-wise." Put a little more simply, the distinction between Father and Son is one of relation, not of substantial characteristics or qualities.

The view Augustine articulates there received succinct formulation in the third of the great ecumenical creeds, commonly known as the Athanasian Creed, which affirms the equality of the three divine "persons" in a series of rhythmic assertions. Uncreated is the Father; uncreated is the Son; uncreated is the Spirit. Father, Son, and Spirit are likewise said to be infinite—and eternal, and almighty. "And yet," as the Creed puts it, "there are not three eternal beings, but one who is eternal; as there are not three uncreated and unlimited beings, but one who is uncreated and unlimited." We do not distinguish among the three persons by pointing to any qualities or capacities, and yet, we must distinguish them. How? Only in terms of the relations that mark their shared history—relations of begetting and proceeding.

What, then, does it mean to speak of a person? Put most simply, a person is, Robert Spaemann says, a distinctive "someone," not a "something." A "something" would be distinguished by the properties it possessed; a "someone" is distinguished by its history of relationships. A "someone," then, is not interchangeable with any other; its distinctiveness is a matter not of qualities but of relations.

The first followers of Jesus were, of course, committed Jewish monotheists; yet, they found themselves responding to the risen Christ in ways they previously would have responded only to Israel's God—in prayer, praise, and worship. They believed that through his Spirit Jesus continued to be present in and with them. So while they continued to believe in one God, they told a story in which that God was named three ways—distinguishing the persons while affirming their coequal divinity. The individual persons are never alone; they are always in relation in community.

That this is a great mystery Christians would not deny. But the mystery is not just about the being of God but about what it means to be an individual person. Augustine affirms the mystery in a passage at which one cannot help smiling. "When," he writes, "you ask 'Three what?' human speech labors under a great dearth of words. So we say three persons, not in order to say that precisely, but in order not to be reduced to silence." Each person is marked by what the philosopher John Crosby calls an "incommunicability" or an "unrepeatability." Those who knew and loved Socrates, Crosby writes,

> will insist that there was in Socrates something absolutely unrepeatable, they will say that there was a mystery of the man and that Socrates was not a mere instance or specimen of this mystery but that he *was* this mystery, so that a second Socrates is strictly, absolutely impossible. When Socrates died, a hole was left in the world, such that no subsequent person could possibly fill it.

In each of those unrepeatable persons we seek to discern a dignity that we should attempt to honor. This is not a destructive individualism; it is the sober truth of who we are before God. Distinctive, singular, and unrepeatable as each of us is, none is ever an isolated individual, and individualism does not have the last word. For to be a person is to be a someone who exists always in relation; it is to be an individual who is never alone.

BIBLIOGRAPHY

Augustine, Saint. *The Trinity*. Translated by Edmund Hill. Brooklyn: New City, 1991.

Beecher, Henry K. "Ethics and Clinical Research." *New England Journal of Medicine* 274 (1966) 1354–60.

Crosby, John F. *Personalist Papers*. Washington, DC: Catholic University of America Press, 2003.

Jonas, Hans. "Philosophical Reflections on Experimenting with Human Subjects." In *Philosophical Essays: From Ancient Creed to Technological Man*, 105–31. Englewood Cliffs, NJ: Prentice-Hall, 1974.

Lewis, C. S. *Miracles: A Preliminary Study*. New York: Macmillan, 1947.

———. "The World's Last Night." In *The World's Last Night and Other Essays*, 93–113. New York: Harcourt Brace Jovanovich, 1960.

Nagel, Thomas. *The View from Nowhere*. New York: Oxford University Press, 1986.

Niebuhr, Reinhold. *The Nature and Destiny of Man*. Vol. 1, *Human Nature*. New York: Scribner's, 1964.

Robinson, Marilynne. *Gilead*. New York: Farrar, Straus and Giroux, 2004.

Schneewind, J. B. "The Divine Corporation and the History of Ethics." In *Philosophy in History*, edited by Richard Rorty, J. B. Schneewind, and Quentin Skinner, 173–91. Cambridge: Cambridge University Press, 1984.

Schultz, Bart. *Henry Sidgwick: Eye of the Universe; An Intellectual Biography*. Cambridge: Cambridge University Press, 2004.

Sidgwick, Henry. *The Methods of Ethics*. 7th ed. Indianapolis: Hackett, 1981.

Spaemann, Robert. *Persons: The Difference between "Someone" and "Something"*. Translated by Oliver O'Donovan. Oxford: Oxford University Press, 2006.

Index